Decorative Aquaria

The Beginner´s Tank

Ulrich Glaser sen.

Acknowledgements

Photos:

We would like to thank the following specialists, companies, breeders and hobbyists for their advice and kindly letting us use their slides. We also thank all those we might have forgotten.

Horst Linke	**Mark Smith**
Marie Paul &	**Frank Teigler**
Christian Piednoir	**Uwe Werner**
Erwin Schraml	**Christian Wyrich**
Archiv A.C.S. Nakano	

Aquarium Glaser GmbH:
for providing beautiful fish for our photographers from their weekly imports

amtra - **Aquaristik GmbH:**
for providing furnished aquaria and equipment for testing

Veterinary consultant:
Dr. med. vet. Markus Biffar,
veterinarian, fish specialist

Die Deutsche Bibliothek - CIP-Einheitsaufnahme

AQUALOG: *Special* - **Serie Ratgeber**
Mörfelden-Walldorf: A.C.S.
Dekorative Aquaria -The Beginner`s Tank - 1998

Dekorative Aquaria -The Beginner`s Tank
Ulrich Glaser sen. - Mörfelden-Walldorf: A.C.S.
(Aqualog)

ISBN 3 - 931702 - 39 -1
NE: Glaser, Ulrich sen.

© **Copyright by:**   Verlag A.C.S. GmbH
Rothwiesenring 5
D-64546 Mörfelden-Walldorf
Germany

Author:
Ulrich Glaser sen.
Scientific consultant:
Frank Schäfer, Dipl. Biol.
Translation:
Andrea Göpel, M.A.
Index und organisation:
Wolfgang Glaser
Editor:
Frank Schäfer, Dipl. Biol.
Cover layout:
Gabriele Geiß, Frankfurt/Main

Print, typesetting, processing:
Lithographics: Verlag A.C.S.
Prepress/Photo processing and graphics:
Michael Blügell, Dipl. Wirt. Ing. (FH)

Print: Giese-Druck, Offenbach
Printed on EURO ART,
100 % chlorine free paper

Further useful tips about care and maintenance can be found every six weeks in AQUALOGnews, the unique newspaper for all friends of the hobby.

Read, for example, the latest breeding reports in the news. It is available in German or English and can be obtained at your local pet shop or subscribed to at the publisher. Order your free specimen copy!

Further literature references on page 47 in the back of this book.

Publisher's address:
Verlag A.C.S. GmbH
Liebigstraße 1
D-63110 Rodgau
Tel.: +49 (0) 6106 - 64469 - 1
Fax: +49 (0) 6106 - 64469 - 2
E-mail: acs@aqualog.de
http://www.aqualog.de

PRINTED IN GERMANY

Cover Photos
Titelphoto: Archiv Verlag A.C.S.

Inhalt

The Author

Ulrich Glaser sen.

He spend his youth (Mr. Glaser was born in 1937) trying to get through the awful times following WW II as best as he could. Of course, his mother was concerned with getting herself and her family through these times of poverty and hunger and there was neither time nor opportunity to get interested in any kind of 'hobby'. Taking up studies at university was simply impossible.

Owing to the circumstances, Ulrich Glaser's first contact with the aquarium hobby was finally made in a pet shop. There, he learned absolutely anything one needs to know about keeping ornamental fishes, from cleaning tanks to breeding rare and precious species. Today, he is looking back on years and years of aquarium and fish tending - a very experienced enthusiast he is indeed.

After having managed several ornamental fish wholesale companies, he founded his own business, together with his wife and his two oldest children, in 1984: Aquarium Glaser, today Europe's biggest ornamental fish import/export company. The firm is now managed by his daughter and has gained a lot of respect in the ornamental fish business.

A few years later, a second branch developed from the fish wholesale company: amtra-Aquaristik, managed by his older son. amtra-Aquaristik produces the well-known amtra products which are sold world-wide.

Still being involved in the import/export business, Ulrich Glaser often found it extremely difficult, if not impossible to identify newly imported fishes - there simply was no useful identification literature available. Out of this unsatisfactory situation the idea developed to start an identification catalogue series: the AQUALOG was born.

In 1995, Ulrich Glaser founded Verlag A.C.S., together with his younger son. The biologist Frank Schäfer, taking over the task of scientific editor, completed the AQUALOG team.

Our team has set itself the goal to catalogue all known ornamental fishes of the world and publish reference books with high-quality, multi-coloured photographs. There are - approximately - 40000 fish species and we have a long way to go if our task is to be realised. But we think, friends of the hobby and specialists alike will appreciate our work.

In order to keep the AQUALOG series handy and easily comprehensible, each book treats one group or genus of fishes. The most beautiful and popular species are shown on an extra poster and are introduced in this Special series. All species belonging to each group or genus, including all varieties and breeding forms, are presented in the respective AQUALOG book.

All AQUALOGs can be supplemented which means that pictures of newly discovered or bred fishes can be stuck in the free pages in the back part of the book. This way, the owner of an AQUALOG can - easily and cheaply - keep the catalogue up-to-date for years and years.

Also, we developed a genuine code-number-system that labels every single fish species and its varieties with an individual code-number. The fish keeps this number even if some day its name is changed. The individual code-number makes every fish absolutely distinctive and internationally communicable, leaving language barriers behind.

Wolfgang Glaser

Preface

How thrilling is the interesting aquarium hobby? How do I prevent mistakes when setting up my first aquarium? How can I furnish it to be natural and decorative?

The AQUALOG advisory series "Decorative Aquaria" with its easily understandable texts, many pictures and drawings shows the best way to reach this aim.

The novice in the wonderful aquarium hobby gets a precise step-by-step explanation, so that he can enjoy his new aquarium right from the start. But also the advanced aquarist might get some good hints concerning equipment, care, diseases and breeding.

These specials are written exclusively by specialists who enjoy to offer advice to the reader out of their long year experience with the aquatic world.

This volume no. 11, of the successful AQUA-LOG-*Special* series attends to a sensible equipping of a "junior tank". At the same time, it demonstrates which fish are best suitable for such a tank.

This manual provides precise instructions for the care and maintencance of fishes and plants. It gives the reader advice what to do when diseases break out or even how to prevent them.

It also contents tips and tricks concerning the breeding of ornamental fish.

On pages 26 to 28, you find a selected choice of fishes we suggest for a beginner's tank.

Besides the pictures integrated in the written parts of the book, we provide you with a variety of fantasic fish photos on the decorative poster supplementing this volume. It shows you a wide range of fishes for an aquarium for beginners.

In the captions, you not only find the precise scientific name of every fish but also the name used in the trade, the so-called common name both in German and English.

You also get to know about the origin of the fish, if it is a wild or a breeding form and which size it can reach. Furthermore, you get informed about all characteristics of the fish, the conditions for its care and also about the size the aquarium has to be.

These information are provided by symbols which are easy to understand and which are explained on page 48 of this volume.

We would like to express our very special thanks to the photographers and all those who helped to make it possible to publish a volume containing such profound knowledge. We hope you will have a lot of fun when reading the book and that it may be helpful to you in setting up and maintaining your first aquarium.

The AQUALOG-Team

Wolfgang Glaser

Basics:
The aquarium hobby - the most beautiful hobby imaginable

In the success-orientated society of today and with more and more people under stress, the longing for a relaxing contrast program becomes more and more intense. Television networks try to satisfy these needs and therefore integrate more and more features about nature and wildlife in their actual programmes.

But many people are already confronted with screens at work and therefore the question comes up if television or computer games are really suitable means for relaxing after a hard working day.
Like no other hobby, an aquarium satisfies men's yearning for his own piece of nature. Fishes are no cuddly toys and one cannot even pet them, but together with an aquarium they form a genuine landscape in the home.

At no other place one can observe fish and aquatic plants in a better way than in an aquarium. This might create a renewed understanding for the relationships in nature and might bring back a knowledge which has been nearly lost by the ongoing civilisation of human mankind. Life underwater is somewhat alien to us but with the help of an aquarium one can observe interesting things that have before been entirely left to divers.

The beginnings of the aquarium hobby date back to the end of the 19th century. At that time travellers brought the first small coloured fishes from far exotic countries back home and sold them to upraise their income. The interest in those exotic animals was immense. Already for a thousand years, ornamental fish have been known in China. But this has not been 'aquarium hobby' in its real sense. At big festivities, brightly coloured goldfish and colour-carps were taken out of their ponds and were put into stoneware pots and vases, so that they could be observed and admired by visitors.

At the beginning, it was not very easy for aquarists, because there were no pet shops and tanks and equipment needed had to be build more or less by the hobbyists themselves. Because of the long ways of transport the fish often were in poor condition and there was not much knowledge about their origin, owning and behaviour. The problems of these experimental times including the men messing around with water in their homes, didn't make the wives too happy, so that most of them were rather sceptical towards the aquarium hobby.

But all this now is history and today, a decorative aquarium is a nice eye-catcher and fits in every apartment. This might be the reason why the number of female aquarists is steadily increasing throughout Europe.

And, thank god, goldfish being imprisoned in glass 'balls' also belong to the past. Today, small fishes of every colour, mostly from tropical parts of the world are rompling about in nicely decorated aquariums which correspond with the needs of their inhabitants.

Turning away from the former glass cases to the decorative aquaria of our time, the aquarium hobby developed into an ambitious hobby.

More and more people get interested in the hobby and therefore the number of aquarists in Europe alone is estimated to be forty millions. Of all hobbies which are somehow connected with animals, the aquarium hobby is the one most easy to handle. When you have a dog, a bird or a cat you need friends to care for them when you are not at home. An aquarium, on the other hand, you can leave alone without problems for a weekend or so.

Most fish have too much weight anyway and some days of diet will be good for them. If you are away from home for a longer time you can purchase a good automatic feeder with an integrated timer at your pet shop. A decorative aquarium is not only a nice looking eye-catcher in your flat but also a pleasure for your whole family.

Even doctors recommend the aquarium hobby to patients who are under stress.

The silent underwater world radiates an agreeable harmony and has a soothing effect on tensed nerves. Still, the observer of an aquarium never gets bored, because there is always something new to discover. He might observe fish mating or taking care of their brood or just some new leaves growing on the aquatic plants.

Basics:
The best place for an aquarium

-Fishes are not impersonal, silent and cold as some people suspect. They don't keep their owners company as other pets do, but with good care they get to know their owner quickly and become friendly, they even take food from his hand.

The most fascinating aspect is to observe how they live together in their habitat. It becomes really thrilling when they form couples. Most ornamental fish show slender and tenacious courtship displays and loveplays.

In an aquarium a lot of fish have a far higher life expectancy than in the wild. With good care a *Paracheirodon axelrodi* can become 10 years old while in the South American areas where he appears most of his clade gets eaten by birds and other animals during the dry season.

When the rainy season begins, thousand millions of young fish hatch out of the eggs which have been laid.

But how can we create an artificial home where our fish feel comfortable?

Nowadays, the often cited 'watermess' which doesn't make housewives too happy does, thanks to the advanced technology, belong to the past. But even today some water changes are needed. We will come to that later.

The fascinating underwater world of the aquarium is a miniature biotope where the various biological processes have to be well-balanced with each other. This is necessary to make fish and plants feel comfortable in their surroundings.
The basic knowledge of how a near-to-nature underwater landscape is established we do explain to you on the following pages.

The size of the tank depends on the room which is available. But there is a rule of thumb which one should follow: the bigger an aquarium, the easier its care.

But nevertheless one can also use small tanks from 60 to 80 cm length or even very small aquaria like "Piccolo" made by Saccem.

For this size only small fish are suited, but there are many species that measure only three to four centimetres when they are fully-grown.

Being responsible for the living animal, the number and size of fishes have always to correspond with the size of the aquarium.

On the following pages, we will show the beginner how to reach this aim best.

At the beginning, the most important question is always where to place the tank.

Obviously, one cannot take any aquarium, put it somewhere and just throw fish and plants inside. It isn't that easy and would be irresponsible towards the living creature. Furthermore the pleasure with it would not last long.

One should always have in mind, that oneself creates a little piece of nature and that the owner of an aquarium is the constructor of a small biotope. But even this makes the hobby such a fascinating one.

To prevent mistakes, some basic knowledge and a systematic approach are needed. This is what we try to impart to you in this book.

The location of your aquarium should not be in direct sunlight. Therefore, a window at the southside of your apartment is not suitable as a location for your aquarium. The consequence would be an enormous growth of algae. In any case artificial illumination is better for an aquarium than sunlight.

Do not put your aquarium near the heating, because the water can be exposed to high variations of temperature.

Otherwise, every place in your apartment is suitable. A socket should be near by. If this is not the case you should ask an electrician to install one .

This is to prevent long cables to fall over. If a new socket has to be installed it should be a triple one, because your aquarium needs electricity for heating, lighting and filter.

Basics:
The different types of tanks

Three impressive aqua-scapes:

Top: A community tank with different cichlids from Lake Malawi, East Africa.

There is a wide range of aquaria to purchase, not only small and big ones. Triangle tanks do fit perfectly in a corner of your living-room. You will also find tanks with high panes which are perfect for the care of angel fish or discus. We would not recommend the so-called column aquaria. They look very decorative but they are unwieldy in care and the fishes look unnatural in these tanks.

Nowadays you can purchase an aquarium in every shape and size you can imagine. You can even construct a whole wall of your living-room as an aquarium by using bullet-proof glass as building material. This gives a most fascinating eye-catcher and when observing it, you feel yourself moved to a far-away exotic country.

Center: A beautiful Amazon tank with majestic discus and tetras.

Your aquarium also can serve as a room divider, but in this case it should have a depth of at least 60 centimetres because it doesn't look too nice if you can see from one room into the other with just few fish swimming around between them. If there's enough space, you can construct a kind of reef in the middle of the tank. This looks fantastic and also is perfect for your fish. Especially for African cichlids such an aquarium with rock-work is the optimal thing.

Bottom: A Tanganyika tank with typical sandy bays, rockwork and plants.

As you see, there are no barriers for your fantasy when it comes to select the shape of your aquarium.

Basics:
The different types of tanks

But you will also see that those special models are much more expensive than the standard tanks you can buy.

The most reasonable tanks you get at specialist pet shops are aquarium sets. They usually have a length of 60 or 80 centimetres. It is an advantage that those sets include already the basic accessories: heating, filter and lighting. This makes it easier, particularly for the beginner, to choose the right equipment. With "super-special-offers" you should be cautious and therefore check if they also offer "super-quality" and if they are proprietary articles.

You also have the possibility to purchase complete-aquaria like the Saccem-"Piccolo" we mentioned before. In this system, heating, filter and lighting are already integrated. This tank contends a water volume of 23 litres and therefore is extremely small, but for 10 ornamental fishes with a size of approximately 2.5 centimetres it is big enough. We tested this itemfor two years and our eight cardinal tetras and two plated catfish felt like a million dollars and the plants as well. The fish stock must always correspond to the size of the aquarium, but we will come back to that later in more detail.

Nearly all aquaria customary in commerce are made of glass. Usually the four side panes as well as the bottom pane are fixed and filled in with a special non-poisonous silicone rubber. Black silicone is the most suitable because it prevents the algae to grow under the rubber filling what can be the case when transparent silicone is used. Algae are able to crack the bond after some time.

You can also find aquaria made of synthetic material or acrylic glass and some of them have a curved front. These kind of tanks have the advantage that they are able to stand a hard punch. Some of them are even described as unbreakable.

We do not recommend those tanks. Our experience has shown that the panes get clouded after some time, You always have a certain amount of algae in an aquarium and to get rid of them you need to use a glass cleaner. If you own an aquarium with synthetic panes it is only a question of time until the first scratches appear.

Basics:
Which aquarium for which fish?

If you want to keep a suckermouth cat or loricariid you cannot use an aquarium of synthetic material anyway. Those fish always search the panes for algae with their rasping suckermouths and the panes become inevitably cloudy. We therefore recommend to buy tanks with at least a front made of good quality crystal glass.

Besides, you can also find square formed tanks, the so-called cube aquaria or as well hexagonal and eight-sided forms which can look very decorative when placed freely in the room.

Our advice is to choose only very big aquaria so that one can hide the technical material in a pile of rocks in the middle of the tank. You will then be able to observe the fish from every

seeds. This gives it a very natural and harmonic look, like a transparent pond inside the living room. Some aquarists were successful in growing new aquatic plants out of the seeds.

Some fish have the habit to jump, some species only sometimes but some in a more extreme way. This must be taken into account when choosing the fish for an open aquarium.

Fish for an open tank should either jump only very little (ca 2-3 cm), rarely or not at all, or the level of the water has to be, like in an paludarium, be much lower than the actual upper edge of the panes.

But lets return to the normal aquarium for the beginner of the wonderful aquarium hobby.

The most common types of aquaria:

Top left: Panorama
Top right: Standard
Bottom left: Hexagon
Bottom right: Delta

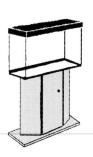
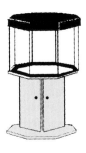
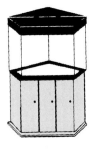

side of the aquarium. Especially the bigger African cichlids do have a fascinating effect in such a tank.

Another wonderful eye-catcher are the so-called paludariums. They can be combined with exotic flowers and other plants and get integrated in a "nature-corner" inside the apartment. You often can find this kind of setup in hotel lobbies. You will find more detailed information about those kinds of aquaria in our advisor "Paludarium".

Those tanks are mostly topless, so that the aquatic plants can grow out of the water and therefore are able to bloom and develop

This is mostly a rectangular glass aquarium out of a serial production.

There are several possibilities. You can purchase a solitary aquarium where you have to add the necessary equipment. A list of all necessary things will be found on the following page.

You also can buy a set which includes the accessories you need. There are also complete aquaria available.

They include (besides the accessories) also a small cupboard, cover and integrated illumination.

Basics:
How to prevent mistakes

Such a combination is a good solution if you don't have something to put your tank on.

For a solitary aquarium you need a robust and waterproof rack.

You can use a shelf, a cupboard or a stand but make sure that it is strong enough to carry an aquarium when it is filled with water.

The weight of the empty aquarium plus substrate and decor plus the quantity of water (1 litre = 1 kg) amount to the total weight.

To determine the water volume use the following calculation:

length x depth x height divided by 1000 = water volume

<u>Example:</u>
You have an aquarium which is 60 centimetres long, 30 centimetres deep and 35 centimetres high.

length = 60 cm
depth = 30 cm
height = 35 cm

L x D x H

60 x 30 x 35 = 63.000

63.000 : 1000 = 63 litres

63 Litres = 63 kg + dead weight
(aquarium/decor) =

ca. 100 kg total weight

A completely furnished 60 cm junior tank weighs astonishing 100 kg!

Basics:
The right equipment

In aquarium sets the stability of the rack has of course been appropriately designed, taking the the total weight of the aquarium into consideration.

Where to place your aquarium is up to your own creativity. It is up to you if you put it lenghtwise or crosswise towards the wall, if you integrate it in the wall unit or if you place it standing free in the room.

It should in any case serve as a nice eye-catcher. But don't forget, it is important that there is always a small gap left in the tank top.

The size of the aquarium depends on the space which is available in your apartment. Never forget the principle: The bigger the tank, the easier the care.

But as we already mentioned, also small aquaria will do. Hereby a second important principle should be taken into consideration: The better the fish match in size and number the aquarium, the more comfortable they feel and the much easier the care will be.

If you are not sure, you better put less fish in your aquarium. You will then have more fun with it. In the following, we start out from an aquarium with the length of 60 centimetres, because this size is the most common offered as a set in the shops.

If you want to have a biggertank, you need to align the details to the higher water volume.

Of course, the instructions for furnishing do not change.

It doesn't make any difference which kind of aquarium you choose, you do need relevant equipment. Part of the equipment is an adjustable heating system to keep the temperature constant.

You also need a good filter to make sure that the water always stays crystal clear. On top of that every aquarium has to have a lighting installation.

It should be brought into line with the volume of the tank to make sure that the water plants can grow and a stable biological balance is reached.

Last but not least you need a good substate where the plants are able to take root and some more 'little helpers' but we will concentrate on that in the chapters to follow.

Some basic tools for aquarium maintenance: net, tweezers, magnifying glass, thermometer and a sieve for live foods.

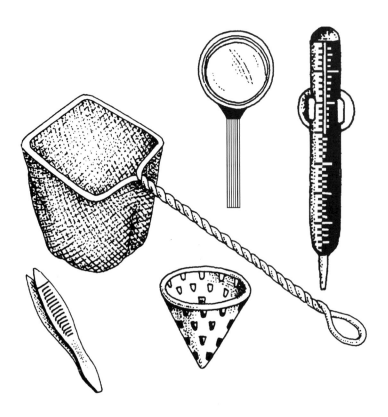

Equipment:
The heating system

In the introduction, we already pointed out that an aquarium should not be situated on an radiator or in direct sunlight, because it would come to high variations of temperature.

That would not be a good idea especially if you want to care for European or North American fish. We would severely advise the beginner of the aquarium hobby against that. The running of cold water aquaria is more lavishing and technically much more difficult than running a warm water aquarium.

Therefore, one should leave the care for such fish and aquatic plants to the specialists. With their long time experience they know better how to handle those animals.

Let us assume that you want to care for tropical fish. In this, the heating is very important.

The trade offers various heating systems. First of all, the well-known pen thermostat heaters. Today, most of them have a protection against overheating and, depending on the model, are fully submersible. You also can purchase heating mats to be installed beneath the aquarium. They might be good for terrariums but we would not recommend them for aquaria because they tend to overheat. To prevent this you need to install a undergravel filter system in your aquarium. This secures a constant water circulation in the ground. You will find further information about that in our advisor "Dutch Plant Aquarium".

You also can find a certain kind of cables which can be heated. They are fixed by suckers on the bottom of your aquarium. This floor-heating proved to be very good, because it stimulates the growing of the plants and the technical material is hidden well.

Most recent development: The combination of the rod-shaped heating and the floor-heating leads not only to a very important circulation of nutriments in the water but also makes the temperature of the substrate rise - you then get healthy looking, lush green plants that grow well.

Nearly all of those modern heating systems are low voltage heaters that are run by a transformer.

If the heating doesn't work properly, no dangerous electric shocks (220 volts) can occur.

It is important that the heating system you buy is adjustable, because you surely don't want to cook your fish. To minimise this danger, the heating power should not be to high. The rule of thumb should be: 0,5 watt per one litre of water volume in the tank. Common rod-shaped heating systems have a small lamp that burns while the heating is in use.

With a sufficient proportient filter you help your aquarium to get what nature reaches with the help of rain, current or bacteria in a pond or a river. In an aquarium you will always find more living things than in a comparable small space in natural inshore waters. For an aquarium you need an additional filter. Well, even a good filter will never have the effect nature has. You will therefore have to change parts of the water from time to time.

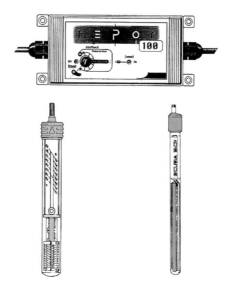

Here we show you the different available heating devices used most commonly in the hobby.

Top: The Tepor-heater is a combination of undergravel and pen heater.

Bottom: Two varieties of pen heaters; that are easily attached to the panes with suckers.

※ Please read the manufacturer's instructions before installation!

But we will come to that in greater detail in the category 'care'.

One of the most important functions of a filter is to make sure that the water circulates and that the gas gets exchanged, at least in small aquaria.

Don't forget to clean your filter because a filter which is just dropping is, of course, useless.

But we will come to that later on page 32.

Equipment:
Filtration and lighting

It would for sure be nonsense to put a big motor filter into an aquarium of 60 centimetres, because it would suck everything out of the water what is not fixed.

So - everything has to be in proportion.

This is an example for the perfect illumination of an open corner tank.

For smaller tanks, you can very well use inside filters with sponges which are pinned up.

These filters work when water is running through the sponge and suspended matters are left inside them.

At the same time, the water is circulating and keeps the water surface moving.

Motor filters running on electricity are available as inside or outside filters.

Mostly they have a high flow speed. In a 60 centimetre tank an inside motor filter takes a lot of space and doesn't look very good when not hidden behind roots, rocks or plants.

Outside motor filters do have the advantage that one can hide them behind the aquarium or below, in the rack.

You have to be careful when the outside filter is on a lower level than the surface of the water.

It is then possible that a hose loosens. In this case your aquarium can run empty and the all the water would be found in the apartment below.

For the beginner owing a small aquarium we would recommend a good inside sponge filter which can be hidden behind the decor.

An inside motor filter which is regulable from 25 - 250 l/h will do as well.

A good lighting is indispensable for your aquarium. Like the filter it has to be in the right proportion to the tank. Here, the rule of thumb should be:

0.5 - 1 watt fluorescent light per litre water volume. If you only have one fluorescent tube, please choose as light colour "daylight/warm-white".

If you use two ore more fluorescent tubes you can add a special plant light tube. Those tubes have an especially reasonable light spectrum.

This is not because with such lighting your aquarium does look better in dark rooms. Also, the aquatic plants need such light conditions to grow.

Plants are not only decor but have an important job to do. They help to reach the biological balance in the aquarium.

When growing, the plants process the carbon dioxide which is formed in the water.

They also produce with the photosynthesis the oxygen the fish need. The plants are only able to grow if they get 10-12 hours light per day.

There are several possibilities of lighting. For aquaria with an open top one uses economical mercury-vapour lamps which hang above the tank.

For a 60 centimetre junior tank, at least for a set, mostly coverings with integrated fluorescent tubes are used.

Equipment:
Beautiful aquaria

Two very pretty varieties of tanks that are furnished with beautiful plants and popular fishes.

Large photo: A swarm of neon tetras (Paracheirodon axelrodi) in a densely planted tank belongs to the absolute evergreens in the aquarium hobby.

Small photo: A lushly planted tank with guppies that impresses with its carefully selected furniture. Such an aquarium beautifully demonstrates how one can emphasize the wonderful colours of these small fish.

Equipment:
Substrate and decor

The right substrate is as important for the perfect aquarium as the heating, the filter and the lighting.

The substrate is the "bio-reactor" of your aquarium. A whole lot of bacteria, fungus and small living things settle in it. Without them a healthy life of animals and plants would not be possible.

It would go too far to go into detail right now, but as a beginner in the aquarium hobby you should know that inside the substrate two basic processes which base on each other take place.

1.) processes by micro-organisms who need oxygen (oxidative processes)

2.) processes which take place under conditions which are low in oxygen (reductive processes).

To make both processes possible, a two-phase construction of the substrate is necessary. Right at the bottom an unwashed layer of a especially for the aquarium hobby developed nutrient substratum, e.g. *amtra* basis plus, (2 - 3 centimetres) is needed.

In this layer the reductive processes we already mentioned take place. They release the nutriment the plants need to survive. On top of that a you have to put a 6 - 8 centimetres layer of loose clean washed sand or gravel.

As a cover you should never use calcareous materials like marble quarry, coral sand or crushed shells. You can do that in a marine aquarium but in here we describe the equipping of a freshwater aquarium.

Those minerals would continuously harden the water and that could be harmful for fish and plants. The best suitable substrates are river gravel, mine gravel or quartz gravel.

Lava or basalt gravel will do as well, but take care that the material you use has no sharp edges because bottom-dwellers like catfishes can get hurt.

For two reasons one should prefer dark substrate : It looks nicer and is better for the fish. Dazzlingly bright substrate reflects incoming light and makes the fish feel uneasy.

Choosing the material for decoration you also have to take care of the amicability. Do never use corals, mussels or other calcium-containing stones in freshwater aquaria. Stones which lock in minerals are harmful as well. Hard wood is without doubt very decorative but it can have sulphur traces.

Make sure that this is not the case. Decor which you have collected in nature must be cooked beforehand, so that all germs are killed. It is even better if you buy your decor at the pet shop.

Little figures made of ceramic like divers, mills, dwarfs, castles, wrecks or treasure chests normally don't belong into a natural aquarium. But this is a questions of taste and especially children (I've been one as well) do like this kind of decor.

Many beginners in the aquarium hobby put such things in the tank but dislike them after a certain time, because the only thing they can observe is the algae growth.

But if you like such decor, feel free to use it. Most of the material they are made of is neutral and therefore they don't harm fish and plants.

Strictly necessary for an aquarium are roots. They are not only decorative but also fulfil important functions as they are a central part of the natural environment and territory of many fish species.

Some fish do rasp the roots because they need the wood as an essential additional food. One can also trim the roots with some plants. That looks very decorative. The trade offers various kinds of roots. You can get savannah wood, mangrove wood iron wood and other. To be able to rasp them, fishes like loricariids need soft wood.

Equipment:
The waterplants

For decoration only you can use hard wood. You should never use roots you collected yourself, except you found them in a moor. A suitable root which you can use for your aquarium has to have laid in the moor for quite a long time. Fresh roots inevitably start to rot when you put them into water and this has, of course, a disastrous effect on the aquarium water. It is much better to rely on your local trader when buying roots for the tank.

We already mentioned that aquatic plants are not only decorative but also take over important jobs in the aquarium. If you buy aquatic plants you should not try to save money.

The plants we describe and show here go together well with all recommended fish of the respective stock group.

They apply to a 60 cm tank, but when you want to start with a bigger aquarium you have to take even more plants of the recommended species, so that the biological balance can be established.

The depicted substrate plan of an exemplary aquarium shows how to place the plants together with the other decor in the most appropriate way.

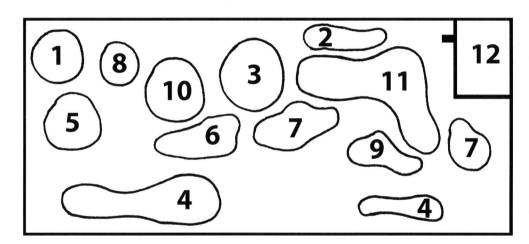

This sketch of a possible tank setup gives an example of how to arrange plants, roots and equipment.

To plant the aquarium thickly is a good precaution against algae, because both groups are nutrient competitors.

The more plants you have in your aquarium, the more nutriments they consume. The less nutriments the algae get, the less they propagate.

It is in any case much easier to put in aquatic plants while equipping your aquarium than add them later because that is more difficult and sometimes turns out to be problematic.

One has to know that there are two different groups of aquatic plants: quick-growing plants and slow-growing plants. For a start one takes al least 2/3 of plants which grow quickly to make sure that no algae problem occurs.

The different numbers symbolise the parts of the bottom which should be planted with a certain kind of plant.

1=*Ceratopteris cornuta*
2= *Hygrophyla polysperma*
3= Amazon swordplant
   (*Echinodorus amazonicus*)
4= *Echinodorus tenellus*
5= *Limnophyla sessiliflora*
6= *Cabomba aquatica*
7= Java fern
   (*Microsorium pteropus*)
8 =*Lagarosiphon major/Elodea crispa*
9 = *Hygrophila difformis/Synema triflorum*
10= *Cryptoryne wendtii*
11= wood
12= filter

Equipment:
The aquarium

We now come to the setting up of your aquarium, provided that you have a tank with all the accessories needed or a set and that you have chosen the right and final location.

The surface on which the tank is set and the underside of the tank now need to be cleaned to prevent uneven patches. Additionally, put a 6 mm strong isolating mat (of styrofoam or the like) under the aquarium to prevent vibrations. Those safety mats are available at every pet shop.

You then take a clean sponge and warm water

Two plants new in the hobby:

left:
Java fern „windelov"

right:
Cryptocoryne cf. walkeri

and wash the inside of the tank properly. You have to do that with a brand-new tank as well, because it is possible that the glass still contains traces of industrial grease.

Be careful not to use any cleanser because even the smallest remains can later destroy your selfmade biotope.

You then place the tank in its final location. Be cautious, everything has to be absolutely clean and don't forget to place the isolating mat underneath. You now fill the tank slowly with water up to the rim and leave it like that for three days.

This is necessary to find out if the rack is really stable; if it is swaying or shaking you have to look for something else to put your aquarium on. When you pour in the water slowly you also will find out if the tank is watertight. Today, the tanks are mostly without any defects, but one never knows and it is better to find out now than later when your aquarium is already fully equipped.

You have already bought substrate , gravel, filter, thermometer, lighting and plants and have also emptied the tank and you now have to install the heating system. If you want to use a submersible heating cable, you have to

The graph explains the division of the tank into three zones (from front to back) by two imagined dividing lines.

start with it now. Take the cable, lay it in a wavy line on the bottom of the tank and fix it there. If you have decided to use a undergravel filter you have to install it now too.

You now fill in the first layer of the substrate. Please do never use potting compost or soil from your garden, that would be of disastrous consequence. You now spread out a 6-8 mm layer of gravel on the substrate . The gravel has to be cleaned before. The best way to do that is to use a sieve and then wash it under the water tap. You can also use a bucket in which you stir the gravel and change the water until it is clear.

When equipping your aquarium with rocks, roots and plants it best comes into effect when you imagine it to be divided into three zones (from front to back) looked at from above.

Mark two imaginary points on second line and one imaginary point on the first line.

You now determine the angle of vision towards the front side from which you will mainly look at your aquarium. Corresponding to this angle of vision you move the points on line 1 and 2 in a way that the rocks, roots and plants, later placed in these positions form an eye-catcher which rises towards the back. The remaining parts of the decor you arrange in a way that the plants and rocks of zone 1 tower up about 5 cm over the substrate . For zone 2 the height should be 10 -15 cm and the plants

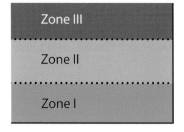

of zone three should be 20-30 cm high. These measures are suitable for an aquarium with the measures 60 x 30 x 30.

In aquaria of other sizes, you calculate one such zone for every 10 cm tank depth.

Equipment:
The aquarium

The substrate is now ready and it should rise towards the back of the tank. That looks really nice and simulates the bank of a pond or river.

It also creates at the front the deepest part of the aquarium, the place where later on mulm can accumulate. That makes it more easy to get rid of it with the help of a syphoning device.

To preserve this landscape from the creativity of bottom-dwelling fish you can lay out terraces by using elongated stones (slate will serve well). They will stabilise the whole thing.

Well, you are now an interior designer and you can decorate the tank according to your own imagination. But don't forget the demands of the future inhabitants.

As already mentioned : Be cautious with mussels, corals, marble and other chalky stones.

Even collected or bought stones should be cleaned and boiled beforehand to kill off germs. This way, you prevent diseases appearing in nature to infest your aquarium.

By using slate, lava or stone wood you should act exactly the same and make sure that no sulphur traces are encapsulated.

By using different kinds of roots you can decorate the tank in a very natural way and additionally create various possibilities for the fish to hide. But take care that beside your wonderful decoration enough place is left for the fish to swim.

As already mentioned you can't use fresh roots because they would rot. For your aquarium you only can use moor pine roots which have rested for many years.

Those moor roots you treat the same way as the stones. Soft roots which are much lighter than hard roots and should therefore be watered longer.

Soaked roots are heavier and stay at the bottom of the tank.

Also, they do not release as much of the tannin that gives your aquarium water an un-

sightly brown colour if you don't waterlog the roots beforehand.

By changing the water from time to time you can support this.

If your aquarium is placed in front of a wall, a background would be not a bad idea.

Different plants suited for a beginner's tank.

left: Vallisneria spiralis

right: Anubias barteri var. barteri

There are inside backgrounds available which contain a low level of harmful substances.
They are, for instance, made of cork but you can also use the ones made by "Back to Nature", a company from Sweden; these items are extremely decorative because of the

left: Echinodorus amazonicus

right: Hygrophila difformis

nature motives they use. You also can find all sorts of outside walls for your aquarium. You usually attach them to the back pane of the tank.

Which one you use is up to you. You also have the possibility to take black cardboard that makes your aquarium look deeper.

We now come back to another important aspect: the heating system.

If you use an undergravel heater it is already installed by now but if you have decided to use a pen thermostat heater, it needs to be installed.

Equipment:
The aquarium

The thermostat heater is attached best in one of the back corners of the tank, using suckers.

This way, it is mainly hidden behind decor and aquatic plants and just the small control lamp is still visible. When you have chosen an inside filter, you can attach it just like that.

You already have installed the technical equipment and filled in substrate, gravel and decor.

Now, fill the tank to the halfway level with lukewarm water. To make sure that the ground doesn't get whirled up, place a small plate on the bottom of the tank and pour the water slowly on it. It is helpful to use a watering can or a hose.

Your underwater garden can now be planted. Put the big plants in the back and place the smaller ones in front of them. You should use a bamboo stick as a holder to make sure that the stems or roots go vertically into the lower substratum layer.

Plastic flowerpots for aquatic plants need to be cut open at the side, so that the roots can grow easier into the ground. It is even better to remove the pots completely.

Don't take too few plants because you want your aquarium to look decorative. Further-more, plants have a very important job: They produce oxygen. On top of that, they provide hiding-places and a room to rest for the fish.

Your garden is complete. Now fill up your tank with lukewarm water (24°C). Before, you have already installed a thermometer and (following the manufacturer's instructions) the outside filter.

You now install the lighting and plug it in.

As already mentioned, the lighting serves an important purpose. Your underwater biotope does look even more fascinating while presented in bright light.

But this is not the only reason for illumination. The plants need the light to grow and to run the photosynthesis and assimilation which produces the needed oxygen.

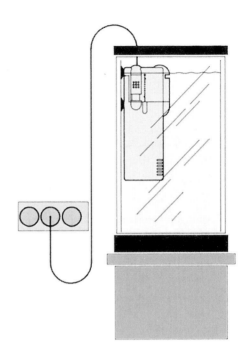

Please read the manufacturer's instructions carefully before installing the heater!

Normally, the customary tank tops include appropriate lamps.

After some time, fluorescent tubes lose their power and thus, should be replaced every year.

For aquaria with an open top the most suitable lights are

- mercury-pressure lamps or

- halogen metal-vapour lamps

which can be fixed above the tank.

They give a good illumination and are econo-mical. When you look at your aquarium now, you will realize that the water is not clear and that it doesn't look as good as the tanks on our nice photos.

But never mind, there will be a change towards good during the next days provided that you did everything right. It is important that the filter is running well and that the water has + 24°C.

But please, do not stock the aquarium with fish right now.

Equipment:
The water

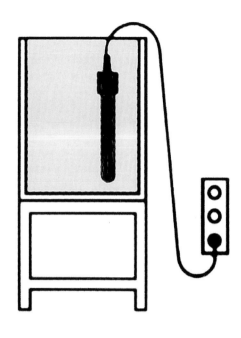

Please read the manufacturer's instructions carefully before installing the heater!

The fry can be damaged by it and young fish can die. Today, copper pipes are commonly used for the warm water supply. Especially in newly build houses the concentration of copper in the water is much higher than in the water coming out of older pipes.

The same effect can be found in new zinc pipes. To avoid the problem you can take the water out of the cold water tap and heat it up to 24°C. It should be obvious by now, that you should never use any decor made of iron, zinc or copper in your aquarium.

So, tap water can be unhealthy for fish and plants. To prevent problems, you can buy several water conditioners, for instance, *amtra* care, at your pet shop. These water conditioners contain substances that neutralize the chlorine which is poisonous for the fish. They also neutralize the dissolved heavy metals. Water conditioned like that also provides a protection for the mucous membrane on the fish's skin and helps them to feel comfortable.

You should know the most important values of the water in your aquarium; most of them, you can even measure by yourself.

Those values include the pH-value, hardness of water, hardness of carbonate as well as the amount of nitrite and nitrate.

You can determine the pH by using test sticks , reagents or electronic testers. To measure the hardness of water or carbonate and the amount of nitrite and nitrate, use the available test kits.

Everything you need is available at specialist pet shops. If you use an electronic tester, don't forget that it needs to be calibrated from time to time. If not, your measurement is inexact.

Be careful with electronic measuring instruments when buying them. The trade often offers cheap instruments, which are often named "toys" by the specialist.

But you also find gauges of high quality, for instance those made by SELZLE. They might be a bit more expensive but will serve you better.

The inside heater should be clipped on the side pane and be submersed completely. Like in all other electric equipment, we recommend to read the manufacturer's instructions carefully before installation.

You better wait another week before you introduce the fish, because first aquarium and filter have to become well-worn. We will come to that on the following pages.

But first we come to the water in general because it is the medium where your fish should feel comfortable.

We don't want to confront you with the wide spectrum of water chemistry because that would only irritate the novice.

Water consists of an incredible lot of components but we first will focus on the metal-combinations. Plants need iron and manganese to grow and therefore parts of it will always be found in fertilizers. Some treatments for fish diseases contain copper-sulphate, but always in a adequate dosage.

You will learn more about that in the chapter "Treatment of diseases".

Copper in a high concentration is deadly for fish. You therefore have to be extremely careful when using water from copper pipes.

Equipment:
The water

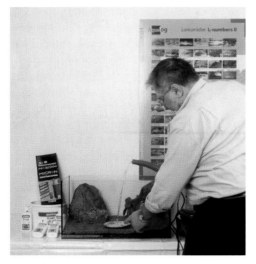

When you find it's too early to buy those things, you can take a sample of the water to your local trader. He will measure it for you and if you are a good client he will even not charge you for that. You should take a well cleaned bottle (do not use any chemical substances for that) and fill it up completely with the water you want to have checked. There must be no air between water and lid.

Water can, depending on the substances which are dissolved in it, be acidic or alkaline. The unit of measurement for the acid content is the pH-value. In nature it can vary from pH 4 to pH 9 which depends on the stretch of water. Water that has an pH of 7 is described by the word neutral. Water with a pH above 7 is called alkaline whereas water with a lower value is called acidic.

You should first measure the water from your tap when it is heatened up to 24°C. Colder water would distort the reading. The water value will not be under 7. The waterworks take care of that, because acidic water would destroy the pipes. If you have a pH-value between 6.5 and 6.8, everything is o.k.

The stocks we recommend in here can cope with that. If the pH is above this range, reaching 8 to 9, you have to treat the water first. You can either use oak-extract or other products.

But this only will work if the hardness of carbonate is not too high. We will come to that in a minute.

The next step is to measure the hardness of water. Rainwater seeps away in the ground and comes out again at another place. During this journey it becomes harder through calcium and magnesium salts that are natural parts of the soil.

Depending on the environment from where the water is obtained and how much of the 'hardening' salts are dissolved in the water, one speaks of soft water (DGH°0,3-10) or hard water (DGH°15-30 or more). In the aquarium hobby another hardness is of importance as well: the hardness of carbonate. In the aquarium the hardness of carbonate is the most important buffer system because it makes sure that the pH-value stays constant.

We do not go into chemical details but it is good to know that in practice you need a carbonate hardness between 4-8°. If the value varies to much please ask your local trader for products to regulate this value.

You now have measured with the help of two different reagents both hardesses (carbonate hardness and total hardness). Normally, the total hardness is higher than the carbonate hardness. If it is otherwise there might be an installation in your house to decalcify the water which replaces calcium with sodium.

If this is thencase,the water is badly buffered and could lead to high variations in the pH-value. This would be damaging for the fish.

If you have measured a total hardness between 5 - 30 and a carbonate hardness between 0.5 - 20 you can use the water. On the poster supplementing this volume you find fish which tolerate these values without problems or which easily adapt to them.

Water with a total hardness of 8 - 15 and a carbonate harndess of 4-8 would be the best to use. If the water has an extremely low carbonate hardness like 0.3 - 3, the pH tends to slide fast into a relatively acidic range. That would not be too good. You can prevent this by using *amtra pH-constant* because it stabilises the pH. If the carbonate hardness of your water is about 8 and if it has a high pH between 7.5 - 8.5 you can try to lower it with the help of *amtra-oak extract* or *amtra trop*.

© Verlag A.C.S. GmbH

Stock:
'Running in' your aquarium

You should also measure the content of nitrite although this dangerous substance should not be measurable when you did everything right while equipping your aquarium.

The excrement of the fish and dead organisms decompose and are transformed by the bacteria located in the substrate and the filter medium into nitrate which is a good fertilizer for the plants.

As you can see, this is no witchcraft. The cycle has to make the creation of a biological balance possible.

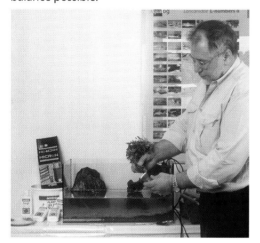

Carefully, plants, stones and roots are arranged.

The plantroots should be free of any stabilising wires and planted vertically into the substrate.

This small amount of food gets the cycle going:

protein $\Rightarrow$ ammonium $\Rightarrow$ nitrite $\Rightarrow$

nitrate $\Rightarrow$ growth of plants $\Rightarrow$ oxygen.

The useful bacteria and micro-organisms can now begin to work.

We do help by providing the right filter and regular care. That means: Good growing plants, not too much stock, no excessive feeding, and regular change of the water.

Well, you found out, drinking water is no fishwater. Useful bacteria and micro-organisms need to settle in your aquarium to keep the cycle running. We call this process "running in" your aquarium.

Hereby you should give a helping hand to speed up the process. You also should "vaccinate" your aquarium.

You best proceed as follows: Firstly you take an appropriate amount of *amtra clean starter* as a biological starter for the filter system.

You then put a pinch of flake food into the water even if there are no fish in it yet.

The 'last act': Attaching the tank top with the included lighting.

Well, one week has passed and you didn't put any fish into you aquarium, even though it was hard for you. But you have for sure observed your aquarium every day and did realise that the plants have grown a bit.

It is now time to control the water values for a last time to make sure that everything is o.k.; and then you can introduce the first fish to your new aquarium.

Stock:
Community tank with different species

In case that you are already an aquarist, we hope that you didn't get bored too much by reading up to now. You might even have found some tips and tricks that are new to you. But let us assume that you are a novice in the aquarium hobby. We therefore have put together groups of fishes which harmonize well. On the enclosed poster you find the fishes and a short description of their most important characteristics.

By now you have finished the measuring and know the values of the water. You can, of course, not go forward now and take any fish out of the recommended stocks and throw them into your aquarium. Not only the water values are important for the fish but also the behaviour of the different kinds of fish towards each other. One cannot put together fishes that fight each other or dispute over the food.

Therefore, we have selected twenty groups of fishes which would be the perfect stock for an aquarium of 60 cm. If you have a bigger tank you can raise the number of fishes. Please use the following rule of thumb: For one fish with the length of 1 cm (fully-grown) take 2 litres of water. But don't forget that fast and much swimming fish need more space. Perches, for instance, should have the possibility to define their territory. On the other hand, you can neglect this rule regarding snails, otocinclus, kuhlii loaches, dwarf cats etc.

Below we provide 20 possibilities how to arrange a stock with a large number of species for your aquarium. We have combined the different fish-societies corresponding to their characteristics and needs. Our long-time experience helped us doing that. All our calculations are based on an aquarium of 60 cm length. If you have equipped a   bigger tank, you can raise the number of the different species accordingly. Do not mix up the different groups, because it is possible that they don't harmonize and this will reduce the pleasure you have with your new underwater biotope.

Stock No.1:

10 Neon Tetras (*Paracheidrodon axelrodi*)
5 Black Neon Tetras
 (*Hyphessobrycon herbertaxelrodi*)
3 Sucker Cats (*Otocinclus*)
2 Corydoras (*Corydoras paleatus*)
2 Hatchetfish (*Carnegiella marthae*)
1 Bristlenose (*Ancistrus*)
4 Ramshorn snails
4 Malayan snails

Stock No 2:

1 Pair of Butterfly Dwarf Cichlids
 (*Microgeophagus ramirezi*)
3 Rummynose Tetras (*Petitella georgiae*)
5 Rosy Tetras (*Hyphessobrycon ornatus*)
5 Black Tetras (*Gymnocorymbus ternetzi*)
4 Sucker Cats (*Otocinclus*)
2 Corydoras (*Corydoras agassizi, C. schwartzi*)
4 Ramshorn snails
4 Malayan snails

Stock No 3:

5 Blue Emperors (*Inpaichthys kerri*)
5 Red Tetras (*Hyphessobrycon flammeus*)
3 Short-striped Penguins (*Thayeria obliqua*)
3 Hatchetfish (*Gasteropelecus, Thoracocharax*)
1 Clown Sucker (*Peckoltia pulcher*)
4 Sucker Cats (*Otocinclus*)
2 Corydoras (*Corydoras agassizi, C. schwartzi*)
4 Ramshorn snails
4 Malayan snails

Stock No 4:

3 Angelfish (*Pterophyllum scalare*)
 (different colours: marble, golden, black)
1 Pair of Butterfly Dwarf Cichlids
 (*Microgeophagus ramirezi*)
3 Yellow-banded Moenkhausias
 (*Moenkhausia sanctaefilomenae*)
3 Black-lined Tetras (*Hyphessobrycon scholzei*)
1 Bristlenose (*Ancistrus*)
2 Corydoras (*Corydoras agassizi, C. schwartzi*)
4 Ramshorn snails
4 Malayan snails

Stock No 5:

3 Blue Congo Tetras (*Phenacogrammus interruptus*)
3 Redeye Tetras (*Arnoldichthys spilopterus*)
1 Pair of Egyptian Mouthbrooders
 (*Pseudocrenilabrus multicolor*)
2 African Glass Catfishes (*Eutropiellus buffei*)
2 Siam Algae Eaters (*Epalzeorhynchos siamensis*)

Stock:
Community tank with different species

Stock No 6:

2 Upside-down Cats (Synodontis nigriventis)
2 Lyretail Lamprologus (Neolamprologus brichardi)
1 Pair of Ornate Julies (Julidochromis ornatus)
5 Clown Loaches (Botia macracanthus)

Stock No 7:

8 Zebra Danios (Brachydanio rerio)
2 Celebes Sunrayfish (Telmatherina ladigesi)
1 Pair of Black Ruby Barbs (Barbus nigrofasciatus)
2 Cherry Barbs (Barbus titteya)
2 Indian Glass Catfishe (Kryptopterus bicirrhis)
1 Black Retail Shark (Epalzeorhynchos bicolor)
4 Kuhlii Loaches (Pangio sp.)
4 Ramshorn and 4 Malayan snails

Stock No 8:

5 White Cloud Mountain Minnow
        (Tanichtys albonubes)
5 Neon Tetras (Paracheirodon innesi)
5 Head and Tail Lights (Hemigrammus ocellifer)
2 African Underwater Dwarf Frog
        (Hymenochirus boettgeri)
4 Sucker Cats (Otocinclus sp.)
3 Pygmy Corydoras (C. hastatus, C. pygmaeus)
4 Ramshorn and 4 Malayan snails

Stock No 9:

8 Neon Tetras (Paracheirodon innesi)
5 Pencilfish (Nannostomus beckfordi)
5 Emperor Tetras (Nematobrycon palmeri)
2 Albino Corydoras (Corydoras aeneus)
4 Ramshorn and 4 Malayan snails

Stock No 10:

8 Glow Light Tetras (Hemigrammus erythrozonus)
3 Starfleck Tetras (Pristella riddley)
3 Bleeding Heart Tetras
        (Hyphessobrycon erythrostigma)
3 Rosy Tetras (Hyphessobrycon bentosi)
2 Corydoras (Corydoras arcuatus)
4 Ramshorn and 4 Malayan snails

Stock No 11:

3 Blood Tetras (Hyphessobrycon callistus)
3 Lemon Tetras (Hyphessobrycon pulchripinnis)
3 Gold Tetras (Hemigrammus rodway)
3 Yellow-banded Moenkhausias
        (Moenkhausia sanctaefilomenae)

2 Corydoras (Corydoras metae)
4 Ramshorn and 4 Malayan snails

Stock No 12:

3 Bleeding Heart Tetras
        (Hyphessobrycon erythrostigma)
5 Redfin Glass Tetras (Prionobrama filigera)
3 Splash Tetras (Copella arnoldi)
3 Silver Hatchetfish (Gasteropelecus sternicla)
2 Corydoras (Corydoras paleatus, C. aeneus)
3 Sucker Cats (Otocinclus sp.)
1 Pair of Bristlenoses (Ancistrus dolichopterus)
4 Ramshorn and 4 Malayan snails

Stock No 13:

5 Sumatra Barbs (Barbus tetrazona)
5 Zebra Danios (Brachydanio rerio)
3 Rosy Barbs (Barbus cochonius)
1 Black Redtail Shark (Epalzeorhynchos bicolor)
3 Siam Algae Eaters (Epalzeorhynchos siamensis)
1 Zebra Loach (Botia striata)
3 Black Ruby Barbs (Barbus nigrofasciatus)

Stock No 14:

1 Pair of Pearl Gouramis (Trichogaster leerii)
1 Pair of Blue Gouramis
        (Trichogaster trichopterus sumatranus)
1 Pair of Golden Gouramis (Trichogaster "Gold")
1 Pair of Dwarf Gouramis (Colisa lalia)
2 Siam Algae Eaters (Epalzeorhynchos siamensis)
4 Kuhlii Loaches (Pangio sp.)

Stock No 15:

3 Yellow-banded Moenkhausia
        (Moenkhausia sanctaefilomenae)
1 Pair of Rainbow Cichlids (Pelvicachromis pulcher)
1 Pair of Egyptian Mouthbrooders
        (Pseudocrenilabrus multicolor)
2 Corydoras (Corydoras agassizii)
1 Clown Sucker (Peckoltia sp.)
4 Ramshorn and 4 Malayan snails

Stock No 16:

5 Yellow-banded Moenkhausias
        (M. sanctaefilomenae)
1 Pair of Flag Cichlids (Laetacara curviceps)
1 Pair Firemouth Cichlids (Thorichthys meeki)
5 Sucker Cats (Otocinclus sp.)
1 Pair of Bristlenose s (Ancistrus dolichopterus)
4 Ramshorn and 4 Malayan snails

Stock:
Community tank with different species

Stock No 17:

5 Harlequins (*Rasbora heteromorpha*)
1 Pair of Paradise Fish (*Macropodus opercularis*)
1,3 (1M+3F) Siamese Fighters (*Betta splendens*)
different colours only 1 male and real females
3 African Underwater Dwarf Frog
    (*Hymenochirus boettgeri*)
2 Siam Algae Eaters (*Epalzeorhynchos siamensis*)
3 Kuhlii Loaches (*Pangio* sp.)
4 Ramshorn and 4 Malayan snails

Stock No 18:

5 Veiltail Guppy "King-Cobra-Gold" Females
    (*Poecilia reticulata*)
3 Veiltail Guppy Males (*Poecilia reticulata*)
3 Coral Red Platys (*Xiphophorus maculatas*)
5 White Cloud Mountain Minnows
    (*Tanichthys albonubes*)
3 (1M+2W) Red Swordtails (*Xiphophorus helleri*)
3 Kuhlii Loaches (*Pangio* sp.)
2 Siam Algae Eaters (*Epalzeorhynchos siamensis*)
4 Ramshorn and 4 Malayan snails

Stock No 19:

2 Upside-down Catfish (*Synodontis nigriventris*)
5 Albino Ice-Blue Malawi Cichlids (2M+3W)
    (*Maylandia greshaki* "Albino")
1 Polkadot African Catfish (*Synodontis angelicus*)
2 Siam Algae Eaters (*Epalzeorhynchos siamensis*)

Stock No 20:

1 Pair of Red Platies (*Xiphophorus maculatus*)
1 Pair of Black Mollies (*Poecilia sphenops*)
1 Pair of Sailfin Mollies (*Poecilia velifera*)
1,2 (1male+2 females) Mexican Swordtails
    (*Xiphophorus helleri*)
2 Siam Algae Eaters (*Epalzeorhynchos siamensis*)
4 Ramshorn and 4 Malayan snails

You now have enough possibilities to stock your aquarium. Choose the suggestion which you like best. I promise: You will have fun with your aquarium right from the start!

Four beautiful fishes we recommend for your first tank.

Top left:
Flame Tetra,
Hyphessobrycon flammeus
(stock suggestion 3)

Top right:
Peppered Cory,
Corydoras paleatus
(stock suggestion 1)

Bottom left:
Red-eyed Characin,
Arnoldichthys spilopterus *(stock suggestion 5)*

Bottom right:
Boehlke's Penguin,
Thayeria boehlkei
(stock suggestion 3)

Stock:
Selecting the fishes

I'd like to make a few remarks on snails. They are not part of every suggestion for the fish setup because some fishes are skilful snail eaters. Some aquarists claim that snails transmit diseases which might be the case when wild snails are collected from ponds by the hobbyist himself. But you have to remember that diseases can also be transmitted via stones or plants that are collected from ponds.

From our point of view, we can say that snails are usually very helpful in aquaria as they feed on food left-overs and are lovely to look at. They do reproduce very quickly, though, and can get out of control very easily. When this happens, the majority of the snails have to be removed from the tank. This is easily done: Put 2-3 food tablets on a small plate, place it on the tank bottom and switch off the lighting for about half an hour. When the lights are switched on again, you will see that many snails have gathered on the plate for feeding - now they can be removed without any problems. Offer your "extra" snails aquarists you know, maybe they are glad to get some.

The fishes listed at the end of every suggested setup are mostly bottom dwellers. They are not only interesting tank inhabitants but also good aquarium "cleaners" as they feed on left-overs and algae. The latter is not done because these fishes want to please their owners but because algae are an essential part of their diet. Algae will grow in every aquarium even if you didn't place it - as we recommend - directly in the sun. This is a natural process and easily restricted by algae-eating fishes.

If an unusual algae growth that cannot be handled by the fishes takes place in your aquarium, something is wrong with the water. Please measure all relevant water parameters and try to find out whether you followed all the guidelines of this advisor.

Glass brushes for cleaning the panes are available at every pet shop and not expensive and for extreme algae growth, there are pesticides. If you need to you such a pesticide, please be careful that it does not contain any copper because copper is not tolerated by most fishes and plants. Anyway, it is much better to maintain the tank regularly and keep it clean than to use such rather unhealthy chemicals.

Well, now it is up to you: At this stage, you will probably have made your choice which fishes you want to have in your tank; the photos and the poster may have helped you with this -difficult?- decision. The species suggested in this book are available at good pet shops.

Please remember that cheap fish are - most of the time - not necessarily good fish. Healthy, high-quality fish do have their price and no dealer can afford to sell them cheaply because he has to add all maintenance costs that amount until a fish is finally sold. Still, it is much better to buy few expensive but healthy and well-tended specimens - such fish will give pleasure from the very moment you buy them.

The question whether all selected fishes should be introduced to the aquarium at once or it is better to introduce only few specimens and watch how they settle in is a much discussed topic among aquarium specialists.

Basically, there is the rule to put all fish that are added to an established fish community under quarantine in a separate tank for some time. There, they are watched for any diseases that might break out during the quarantine period. Only if they have proved to be healthy they should be introduced to the established community.

If you don't want to set up a quarantine tank in addition to your first 60 cm tank or simply don't have the space for it we suggest that you proceed however you think is best. If you choose the step-by-step method it is sensible to begin with one or two species of the suggested community.

It is very likely that all fishes you buy at the pet shop of your choice are healthy when the first specimens turn out to be in good condition. Usually, it is quite safe to add fishes from the same dealer because most dealers sell animals from the same instalment.

We warmly recommend to stick to the "dealer of your choice". Quality and health are the top priorities in aquarium fish and one should resist all temptations to buy "special offers" - one might risk the well-being of the whole aquarium community.

Stock:
Introducing the fishes to the tank

Cardinal tetras in the usual plastic bag used for transport. Allow the bag water to adjust to the tank water by floating it for about half an hour. This way, unnecessary stress for the fish through rapid a temperature change is prevented.

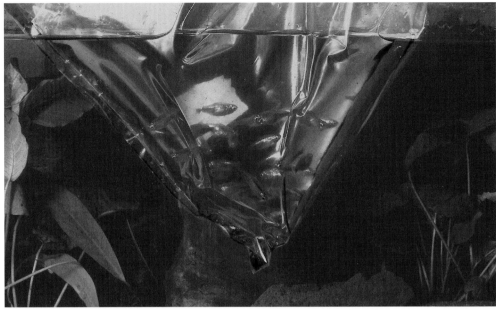

Now, the most exiting moment has arrived. Everything has been checked and is okay. The first fishes are introduced to your new aquarium. The fishes you bought are normally supplied in plastic bags. It is important that the animals do neither cool down too much (in winter) nor heat up (in summer) on the way home; this is easily done with an insulated container in which the fishes are transported.

I recommend to watch the dealer how he prepares the plastic bags, because such knowledge can be very useful if you have to do this yourself, because, for example, you move to another home or give away young fish you bred.

In the plastic bag, the fish do not only need water, they also need oxygen - otherwise they would suffocate. As a rule of thumb, dealers add 1/3 oxygen to 2/3 water. If pure oxygen is not available, 'normal' air will do as well, but then you can only carry _ of the number of fish that can be transported in an oxygenated bag.

When you get them home, switch off the aquarium lighting and float the bag about half an hour in the tank so that the bag water can adjust to the temperature of the tank water. Then you can carefully open the bag. If the bag water is clear and not dirty, you can gradually change the bag water for tank water, by allowing some to run into the bag and pouring a little out from time to time.

This way, the water keeps mixing and the bag floating. The whole procedure takes about 30 minutes. If the water is not clear or dirty from excrement, you proceed basically the same way but do not allow the dirty bag water to run into the tank; it is removed with a small cup and poured into a bucket.

Please be careful that during the whole procedure the bag has a sufficient air content.

After half an hour of mixing the water the fish can be transferred to the aquarium: simply release them together with the rest of the bag water. If the rest of the bag water is dirty, pour it carefully into a bucket or large bowl, net the fish and transfer them to the aquarium.

You proceed like this every time you add new fish to an established tank and also when you transfer your first ever fish community from the quarantine tank to their permanent home. In any case, it is most important to slowly assimilate the different waters.

If you decide to use a quarantine tank for the settling in period, you should refrain from decorating it with. Plants and other hiding places would have to be removed from the tank before you could catch the fish - an unnecessary waste of time, and also a rather difficult task when it comes to removing loricariids or kuhlii loaches from their hideouts. For the fish, it would be very stressful, too.

Stock:
The waterplants

For the first few hours, the fishes have to get used to their new environment without any extra lighting.

After this first period of settling in, you can switch an the lighting and enjoy the wonderful and exciting scenery that the little biotope you created presents.

Assumed that everything is all right, the fishes should swim peacefully around the tank. Swarmfish should have formed a group by now, though they are still enquiring every single spot of their new home.

The first feeding can wait until the next day; your pets won't starve within this short time.

Usually, fish get used very quickly to their new environment and accept readily the offered food. Of course, fishes and plants need to be feed according to their needs.

Water plants do not have to be fed on a daily basis, as they obtain most of their requirements from the fish's excreta.

Still, this "food" is not sufficient and thus they have to be additionally fertilised two or three times a year.

When you furnished the tank, you already included a layer of special plant soil that provides nutriments for about five months. After this period, a regular fertilisation is necessary.

A very useful fertiliser is natural tropical laterite like, for example, *amtra* plant laterite balls that are thrusted into the substrate near the plants.

The advantage of this method is that the nutrients now released by the fertiliser can only be used by the plants and not by algae!

You only have to take care that the balls are presses completely into the substrate because only in the reductive milieu the plant can extract the essential iron ions from the laterite.

Such an iron-supplementing fertiliser guarantees healthy, richly green plants. If you use a liquid fertiliser, use it economically as this way you fertilise algae, too.

One way to get really beautiful and lush growing plants is to "feed" the plants with CO_2, carbon dioxide, via a special CO_2 unit.

When exposed to light, plants use carbon dioxide and release more oxygen than they need.

The oxygen surplus is breathed by the fish. Without light, i.e. during the night, plants work the same way all other organisms living in your aquarium do: they use oxygen and produce carbon dioxide.

As the carbon dioxide content influences the pH of the water, it is very dangerous to add CO_2 without measuring the pH constantly.

A sudden change from pH 7 to pH 6 can be deadly for many fish species.

An illustration of an CO_2 installation; different makes are available at pet shops.

Therefore we advise beginners against installing such a CO_2 unit in a 60 cm tank. If you still want to use this kind of equipment, and are not willing to spend a lot of money on a pH regulating unit, you should, at least, buy a rather cheap CO_2 control device that switches the CO_2 supply off during the night.

Maintenance:
The right foods

This chapter is about the right feeding of aquarium fish. In nature, fishes feed on the most diverse kinds of foods. Most fishes are carnivores, i.e. they eat worms, small crustaceans or other small animals. Larger species are very often predators and regard all fish that are smaller than themselves as food.

The next group are the omnivores, fish that eat animal and plant foods, and the limnivores

For the health of our aquarium fishes, additional feeding with the readily available frozen foods is indispensible.

These kinds of food tablets are especially suited for bottom-dwellers like catfishes. Still, some cichlids, like this mouthbrooder from Lake Victoria, also enjoy feeding from the ground.

that graze off the surfaces of plants and roots or stones, thus eating plants and micro-organisms.

Thirdly, there are the herbivores, fish that live exclusively on a vegetarian diet and that can sometimes be dangerous for your aquarium plants when not sufficiently fed.

Further, there are species that are specialised and need certain foods to survive, like some of the popular armoured catfishes which need to rasp wood of certain roots as a supplementary food. For such food "specialists" soft roots have to be integrated in the tank furniture.

There's no need to feel uncomfortable now - we intentionally left out all species that require such special care and attention in this advisor. All fishes recommended in here do fine on the usual foods you can buy at pet shops. The storage of live tubifex in the refrigerator is also one the more unpleasant facets of the aquarium hobby that belong - fortunately - to the past. Today, all pet shops offer a wide variety of live and other foods for aquarium fish.

For bottom feeders, tablet food is available, fish that feed more in the top or middle

regions of the tank, flake foods can be recommended. There are freeze-dried mosquito larvae and tubifex in different packages and forms (e.g. tablet) as well as frozen foods packed in single portions for the "gourmets" in your aquarium. Except from live foods, frozen food is the most "natural"; it should be fed regularly, at least as a supplementary part of the fish's diet. Like in all other aspects of fish keeping, quality is very important. Cheap foods often come from polluted waters and can bring in harmful substances and diseases. Fish foods should not be stored too long. We thus recommend all keepers of 60 cm aquaria to buy small packages even if they are a little bit more expensive than the large ones. If you buy the foods at your local pet shop, you can be sure that they are always fresh.

There are fish species that can only be settled in with the help of living, moving food. We left these fishes, like all other food specialists, out of our fish community recommendation.

Anyway, these kinds of fishes are usually adjusted to the common aquarium foods by the importer and the dealer before you buy them. Now you know the different kinds of food that are usually preferred by ornamental fishes. If you follow this advisor step-by-step, you did not feed your new pets immediately after introducing them to their artificial biotope but waited until the next day. And now, the exciting moment has come when your fishes are fed for the first time: Give a little flake food to the tank (a tip of a knife is enough) and see what's happening.

In feeding aquarium fish, there is an old rule of thumb: Feed only so much food at one time so that practically all of it is eaten greedily within a few minutes.

Maintenance:
Feeding

In the very first feeding your fish will not pounce upon the offered food as they will do when they are used to the feeding "ritual", i.e. when they know the time and the place. If

they do nevertheless, it is a good sign and proves that everything is okay and the new environment accepted.

This is another important rule: When your fish eat readily and greedily they are - usually - healthy and feeling well. You should observe, though, if the food is eaten and swallowed and not spat out again.

When your fish show the latter behaviour, the food could be old. When the fish appear apathetic and do not eat, this is a secure sign that something is wrong: Either the water quality has deteriorated or some kind of disease is about to break out. What to do in the latter case can be read in the chapter about disease treatment.

To feed regularly two or three times a day, and always as much as is eaten immediately, has turned out to be favourable. You have to take care that the bottom dwellers (like cats) get their share, too.

For catfish species it has proven best to give two or three food tablets to the tank after the lighting has been switched off. Ancistrus, armoured catfishes and some other species are nocturnal feeders, but most of the time they get used to the daily feeding times and eat together with their tank comrades.

It might happen that you inadvertently gave much more food to the tank than you intended to.

When such a thing happens, you have to siphon off all remains or you risk the breakdown of the sensitive biological balance in your miniature biotope! Decaying food leftovers can form toxic substances (nitrites). After such an "feeding accident" you should wait until the aquarium water is crystal-clear before you feed again.

Any visible clouding signals that the converting bacteria in aquarium and filter have not yet finished their work and are still busy with eliminating the damage.

There is no solitary food that contains all necessary nutriments and therefore, you should always feed a mixed diet.

Quality flake food as main course, with regular additions of vegetable or meat food tablets and frozen food will soon turn out to be not only healthy for your fish but also enjoyed by them. If you are way for the weekend, it is okay with your fish to stay hungry for this short time.

Fish have the habit to eat more than they really need, thus accumulating a food "store". Their greedy way of eating mostly tempts their keeper to feed more than necessary, anyway, so that, like in nature, the odd fasting day is tolerated without any problems.

Your fish can even stay hungry for several days without any harm; when you are away from home for more than a week, there are the already mentioned automatic feeders available. All foods listed in this chapter (except frozen foods) can be portioned for several weeks and are fed with the automatic feeder.

Please take care that the feeder is only packed with as much food as is really needed during your absence.

The lighting has to be switched on at least 10 to 12 hours a day, so that a time switch (that regulates the automatic feeder, too) is indispensable. Even better is a good friend who comes in regularly and checks that everything is all right:

A electrical breakdown would have devastating consequences for your pets, so that, of course, a good friend or fellow aquarist of good experience is the best "insurance" against any disasters like overfeeding, starvation, suffocation, pollution etc.

Neon tetras are fed with flake food.

Maintenance:
Working in the aquarium

One more thing: while the automatic feeder and the lighting are regulated by the time switch, the heating and the filter have to be turned on all the time.

All requirements of the introduced fishes can be found in the captions on the included poster; easily understandable symbols provide the most important care instructions for each species. Let's now turn to another aspect of fish keeping, the aquarium maintenance.

The most important point of aquarium maintenance is to perform the few, essential measures that have to be taken for an intact environment in your tank on a regular basis. Regular maintenance not only guarantees healthy tank inhabitants but saves time, too.

When fish eat, they do, of course, also release excrement. In nature, the faeces pose no problem, but in a limited area as the miniature biotope "aquarium", the aquarist has to take care that excrement and other deteriorating substances do not endanger the sensitive balance.

Water plants, micro-organisms and bacteria living in the biological filter and the substrate do their share of work in keeping the tank clean. Still, not all processes can be regulated this way, and in a small 60 cm tank, it is even more difficult.

All harmful substances that are dissolved in the water are best removed with a regular partial water change.

There is one golden rule: Never change the complete tank content at once (without a reason) and avoid to replace filter material and change a larger quantity of water at the same time; this would disturb the biological balance in your aquarium completely.

Fishes, plants and micro-organisms alike would be "shocked" and the whole biosystem would have to be established once again.

The usual specialist literature recommends a partial water change of - to 1/3 of the tank content every 2 to 3 months. This can work, but our long-time experience has proved a partial water change of 10 to 15% of the tank content every one or two weeks as favourable.

But - if it has to be carried out so often, how can it be done without a lot of trouble? And how can it be done without making a mess (and without, consequently, having a dispute with other members of the household about the almost unavoidable water stains)?

I recommend to proceed as follows: Before beginning with the water change, place an exactly fitting piece of an old, thick carpet around your tank. This 'carpet cover' prevents the expensive carpet or wooden floor from any damage even if some water is spilled.

Algae might grow on the front glass despite the presence of "algae clearers" like loricariids. Before you start to change the water, remove the algae first with one of the available glass cleaners.

The next step is to unplug the power supply for heater, lighting, filter etc. Then you take a watering can (8-10 l) for the old water and start to siphon 10% of the water with a thin tube.

Using a watering can is more practical as it prevents splashing; also, you can use the old tank water for watering your flowers afterwards.

Begin to siphon at the "dead spots" in the tank where mulm and other debris may collect. Be careful that no curious small fish are sucked into the tube during siphoning.

In order to prevent the typical mouthful of aquarium water that comes unavoidably when you begin the water change with sucking the water into the tube, fill the tube completely with water and hold the ends close with your thumbs.

Put the one end into the watering can, the other into the aquarium, take away your thumbs - and you have an optimal suction. In a 60 cm tank, the 10 to 15% of changed water make about one or two fillings of a watering can.

Now you fill the watering can with new water (ca 24°C), add the recommended amount of water conditioner to it and pour it gently into the tank. And that's it! Don't forget to plug in all power supplies afterwards.

Maintenance:
Working in the aquarium

When cleaning a filter, the procedure differs, depending on the kind of filtration system you have.

If you installed one of the usual sponge filters in your 60 cm tank, you can - despite our warning - clean the filter and change the water in one operation.

Remove the sponge and clean it by squeezing it repeatedly under a strong stream of luke-warm water.

Do not use hot or cold water and don't wash it in washing-machine!

Only the visible wastes are to be cleansed off, not the useful bacteria living in the sponge.

This is also the reason why the sponge must never dry up completely for a longer time.

But sponge filters are the only exception from the rule - other filtering devices must never be cleaned at the same time you make a water change.

In other filters you replace the old filtering media by a new one every 2 to 3 months.

The new media should be rinsed under tap water beforehand.

Old filtering floss is disposed of, other filter media can be flushed clean under a strong stream of water; again, use only lukewarm water.

The filter media that has to be replaced depends, of course, on the make of your filtration system; your pet shop dealer will help you to buy the right replacement items.

After each water change it is recommended to check the water chemistry, because a water change is always an intrusion on the delicate biological balance of an aquarium.

Dead brown leaves of water plants should be cut off with scissors, but that's about it; don't snip at your plants all the time.

Water plants are neither bonsai nor hedges.

Plants like

- *Anacharis (Elodea)*,

- *Ludwigia*,

- *Hycrophyla*,

and - *Myriophyllum*

with a single stem that grow rather long should be pinched back when having grown too long and shading the tank too much.

The cut off pieces can be thrusted into the substrate; there, they soon strike roots and grow.

You can also give the cuttings to a fellow aquarist or maybe furnish a second tank with them.

When you follow all recommendations and maintain your aquarium regularly, the tank will stay clean and "healthy" for many years and a major overhaul won't be necessary for a very long time.

The most basic requirement for this is: not to overfeed your fishes and the correct setting up of the tank in the first place.

Fishes and plants form a well-functioning bio-system that will stay balanced if waste loads are regularly removed so that the invisible little helpers (the bacteria) can do their work and keep the water clean and free of harmful substances.

Maintenance:
Disease prevention

Up to this point, we talked about several aspects of setting up a tank, maintaining it and keeping fishes. Which leaves another basic question open: Can fishes contract diseases despite all efforts?

Well, of course: aquarium fishes, like all other living beings, can fall ill. But when kept at the best possible conditions, they are seldom subject to bad or even life threatening diseases. Most diseases are latent in every organism

and can break out when the organism is distressed in some way, like, for example, through disturbance of the usual way of living or continuous stress.

Or through negative changes of the animal's environment - which leads us, the aquarists, to the water our fishes live in and, again, the importance of constantly controlling the water quality.

Almost all fish diseases that crossed my way in the many years I spend as an aquarium enthusiast were - as far as they were diagnosed and their causes analysed - the result of a deterioration in water quality.

Therefore, it is most important to regularly carry out all necessary steps of maintenance. One of these measures is the regular partial water change which shouldn't be done only when the water is already cloudy and the fishes display signs of distress.

Just imagine, the pH of the water had steadily fallen to pH 4 (because you forgot the water change) and the fishes had slowly adjusted to this pH. If you change water at this stage, using water with an pH of 7.8, you can probably picture the shock fishes and bacteria will get from this procedure.

A similar thing would happen if you changed the whole filtration system at once. The whole bacteria population would be gone, and new bacteria would have to be established.

The break-out of any latent disease will almost inevitably follow. In order to prevent disease break-outs, the frequent measurement of the water parameters should become maintenance routine for any aquarist. The most important reading in a tank is of the nitrite level. Nitrite shouldn't be measurable at all in your aquarium - a level as low as 0.5 mg/l can already be harmful for your fishes.

If such a high nitrite level is measured although the necessary maintenance programme was carried through regularly, one has to search for the reasons for this dangerous intoxication of the aquarium water. Very often, it is caused by excessive feeding, rotting plants, or an overstocked tank.

Also, an ineffective because too weak filtration system can be the reason for the accumulation of nitrite. If, for example, the airlift of an inside filter is too far away from the water surface, the filter only drips or starts to hiccup because the amount of water that runs through the filter is too little.

The following filter media are available:
1 - filter floss
2 - biocell
3 - grid
4 - ceramic
5 - ultra carbon
6- special peat

Maintenance:
Disease treatments

Such technical defects as described above are easily repaired. But what else can you do to prevent diseases?

First of all, one shouldn't, of course, buy any ill fish. Starved specimens with a hollow belly, or obviously ill specimens with cloudy eyes, damaged fins or visible patches of fungus on fins and body have to be left aside. Healthy fish do have their price, please resist any temptation to buy so-called "special offers", because specimens purchased at sales could destroy your whole fish community.

It is possible, though, that even fishes at your pet shop contract diseases, but a conscientious dealer will never sell ill specimens to his customers. But this has already been discussed, just as how to settle in your new pets. Still, there is one more thing I think is important when it comes to disease prevention: You should always buy young, "medium" sized fish. This means, the animals should be not too young, but not fully grown either. It is like in planting a tree in your garden: If it is too small, it might have problems with taking root, if it is too old, it hardly has a chance to adjust, too. And in fishes that have to adapt to a new environment, it is just the same.

When your fishes fall ill despite all prevention, you have to know what to do. Therefore, we will share our experiences with you in the following chapter.

It is essential that you are able to ascertain yourself quickly of the tank inhabitant's condition so that you can detect and diagnose diseases at the earliest possible stage. Only the immediate correct treatment of a given disease can guarantee that ill fishes recover fully.

It should become daily routine to check your fish's health. The best opportunity for the daily check-up is, of course, feeding time. Healthy fishes respond quickly to food in the tank and eat greedily.

If your fishes suddenly display a diminished appetite, lose weight, are apathetic and lethargic, rub themselves or show strained breathing, you know that there's trouble ahead.

Basically, there is no miracle cure for diseases. As this is an advisory handbook, it would be far beyond its scope to discuss all known fish diseases and their treatment. We warmly recommend to buy real specialist books, like, for example, by UNTERGASSER or BASSLEER we listed all books we consider useful in the back of this Special.

Here, we will list only the most common diseases and their cure.

If diseases do appear in a tank, they are mostly fungal skin infections on fins and skin of injuries resulting from being netted in the pet shop or fights among the tank inhabitants.

Usually, such infections heal by themselves and eventually the fungus will fall off. If not, raise the water temperature to 28°C for several days. Now the fungus should heal or fall off.

If one or few larger specimens are infected, they are netted from the main tank and transferred to a small quarantine tank.

Treat the isolated fish as follows: Raise the water temperature, add some iodine-free salt (1 spoon to 10 l water) and a water conditioner. In this conditioned water the fungal infection should heal completely.

If a fish has a healthy appetite but loses weight nevertheless, this could be a sign for worms or the single-celled parasite Hexamita. Both infections can be treated; medications for Hexamita are available at pet shops.

Drugs for treating worm infections are only available in pharmacies with a vet's prescription.

If your fishes display an increased breathing frequency, this could be caused by a technical problem.

Check the water parameters!
Is the water temperature correct? Use a second thermometer!
Is there enough oxygen?
Is the filter working?
Is the water clear or maybe clouded by food left-overs?

When the rapid respiration is combined with symptoms like clamped fins, strange, swaying movements and rubbing against stones or suchlike, the fish is probably infested with parasites.

There is, first of all, the well-known *Ichthyophthirius*, the White Spot Disease or ich; it can be seen and diagnosed quite well with the naked eye. It might be already too late if you see a fish that's completely covered with white spots.

The first sign of a possible infection with ich is a fish that rubs itself against stones or roots or any other objects in the tank.

A soon as you discover white spots where white spots do not belong, you have to react immediately.

With the beginning of any suspicious rubbing or the discovery of any white spots, you should treat the infected fish with a medication, like. for example, amtra medic 1.

Medications for fish diseases are usually available at your pet shop. When used correctly and early enough, the cure should be successful, although water plants are quite intolerant of these substances.

If you have catfishes in your community tank you have to put them into a separate tank and treat them there with a reduced dose. The main tank is then treated with the recommended dose as usual. Please remember: Fish disease medications, like all other medicines, have to be kept away from children!

There is another parasite that is even more than unpleasant: Oodinium or Velvet or rust disease which is rarer but also more difficult to recognise. Infection with this disease manifests itself in form of spots, but much smaller then in ich, and also not white but more grey or velvet:

In the final stage of the disease, the fish is covered with a greyish dust. When this stage has been reached, a cure is nearly impossible. Treatment is with the available drugs containing copper sulphate or with adding high-quality sea salt to the water so that the resulting solution is at a concentration of 1 to 1.2%.

Please note: Many fishes do not tolerate such high salt concentrations. Therefore, you have to observe your fishes closely during the whole treatment period. In order to eradicate all Oodonium parasites, the high salt concentration has to be kept for 5 to 6 days. Then the water should be gradually changed; I recommend a daily change of 10 to 20% of the water to remove the salt from the tank.

Like in ich treatment, water plants do neither tolerate the copper components in the drugs nor the high salt concentrations. But fortunately, these bad diseases are really rare in well-tended aquaria.

As already mentioned, it is beyond the scope of this manual to list all possible fish diseases. When you need help, ask a fellow aquarist of good experience or your pet shop dealer.

There are veterinarians who are indeed specialists for ornamental fishes but, unfortunately, they are very rare. Ask your vet nevertheless, he might have an idea or can recommend a helpful book.

Tips for disease prevention can also be found in the newspaper for aquarists, AQUALOG NEWS that's available every six weeks at your local pet shop. The fish specialist Dr Markus Biffar our "Fishdoctor" gives advice and answers questions from readers.

When diseases occur in your aquarium, don't put the blame on your dealer. No serious dealer will sell ill fish on purpose; he is certainly more interested in having satisfied, long-term customers. In all obviously healthy fish a latent disease can break out when the animal is stressed by the catching or transport procedure. So once again: Put all newly purchased specimens into quarantine before you introduce them to your established fish community.

One more tip for beginners: If you have a pair of Pseudocrenilabrus or any other mouth-brooding species and one of the two does not eat for days but looks healthy, the fish is probably not ill, but carries eggs or even freshly hatched fry in its mouth. During the brooding period, the parent will not eat at all. Which leads us to the next, highly interesting point: the breeding of ornamental fishes in the aquarium.

Breeding:
Basic requirements and tips

Can water plants contract diseases, too? The answer is: Yes, they can. Fortunately, plant diseases are not contagious as fish diseases are and they don't have to be treated with drugs. There might be to odd plant that dies, but also others that grow lusciously. Some water plants "retreat" when ill but grow anew all by themselves after some time.

The most important requirements for healthy plants are sufficient light and nutriments. Light is especially important. When the tank surface is covered by excessively growing stems and leaves or a carpet of floating plants (like duckweed), the plants growing in the bottom area of the tank will surely die of light deficiency.

To prevent such a thing happening, you have to cut back all plants that grow too lush. Duckweed is netted from the surface; the remaining few will quickly reproduce. Some fish species actually eat duckweed as a supplementing part of their diet.

Green algae are harmless but can make the tank unsightly when growing on front or side panes. Blue-green algae can appear as a slimy cover on the tank's substrate, plants or roots.

The growth of these algae results from over-feeding and the deterioration of the left-overs. Beard and brush algae are very often the result of CO_2 deficient water with a too high pH. As soon as the water has the correct parameters the algae problem should be solved, too.

Floating algae turn the water milky-green or so cloudy that it is absolutely opaque. The reason for their appearance is always too intense lighting by sunlight which can be quite easily avoided.

Diatoms appear as a thin brown slime on the aquarium furniture and substrate. They are caused by oxygen deficiency, too much nitrate and too little light. Check the light intensity of your illumination system and whether water plants shade the tank too much.

In all algae listed here the elimination is quite easy. They are a nuisance but don't be bothered too much if they should appear one day in your tank. A secure sign for fishes that feel really well in their artificial biotope is, of course, reproduction. Up to this point, I tried to explain how to find the best possible starting point into this wonderful hobby and what to do to establish a tank that meets all the requirements of your new pets.

Anyway, whether you feel self-confident enough to try to breed your fishes, is completely up to you. In any case, you shouldn't force the breeding activities of your fish as hasty breeding attempts will almost certainly end in failure.

Take your time and observe the fish community closely. Watch your fish intensely and learn how to distinguish the sexes in the different species. In some fishes, this is quite easy as males and females look very different indeed, like in guppies, swordtails and platies.

In other species, like, for example, the Neon tetra or some mouthbrooders, this is much more difficult.

In some species, it is even impossible to detect any distinguishing features: In these fish, you simply have to wait whether pairs form or not.

When breeding is successful, there are different possibilities how the success came about. "Accidental breeding" occurs all by itself and all you do is to detect the offspring in your tank one day. "Hobby breeding" involves you as a "saviour" of the fry, as you net them from the main tank and rear the young in a separate one.

In livebearers, you separate the pregnant female from the community and raise the babies in a rearing tank to prevent them from being eaten by their parents or other inhabitants of the community tank.

In "Professional breeding" the most important goal is to breed two selected specimens with each other, by separating them, spawning them and rearing as many young as possible.

For this, one needs a lot of experience and a suitable installation of several breeding tanks. Still, in no other pet the owner can hope for offspring in such little time, with such little effort and such little space as in aquarium fishes.

Breeding:
Livebearers, mouthbrooders and bubblenest builders

The cichlids of the genus Geophagus *belong to the mouthbrooders. On thi s photo you see a female* Geophagus steindachneri *from Columbia collecting her fry.*

Generally, the reproduction behaviour of fishes is very variable and differs in some groups entirely. This makes observation and studying fishes so very interesting.

We know, that, for example, the salmon (*Salmo salar*) migrates an incredibly long way from the seas where it lives to the rivers where it spawns. The young journey back to the sea, but when the mating season draws near, they return to the place where they were born.

In eels (*Anguilla anguilla*) it is the other way round. For spawning, they migrate from our rivers to the Saragossa Sea at the coast of Mexico. The young "glass eels" (that's what they are called due to their transparent appearance) then swim back the whole way to our European rivers.

Until today, all attempts to suppress this behaviour and breed eels commercially failed. And this in space age! Well, nature holds still its secrets, despite all our efforts to solve them. But let's return to the ornamental fishes. In the aquarium species, there are, of course, also the most different breeding techniques.

Basically, two different kinds of reproduction are distinguished: egglayers and livebearers. In the egglaying species, there are fishes that spray their eggs and forget about them; they do not show any brood caring behaviour.

To this first type, most barbs and tetras are counted. The second type are egglayers that take care of their brood. These fishes are called substrate brooders.

They spawn on some kind of substrate and guard the eggs after they have been fertilised by the male. In this group, there are the open brooders that spawn on stones, plants, roots or even the tank panes, the cave brooders that hide their eggs in cracks in rocks, caves or other secure hiding places and guard the spawn aggressively against any intruders; and thirdly the mouthbrooders that take the fertilised eggs into the mouth where incubation takes place.

This is actually the male's task, but very often, the female takes on "his" work.

In the absolute safety of their mother's or father mouth cavity the eggs and the hatched young stay until they are large enough to have a chance of survival.

Finally, there are the bubblenest builders.

This fascinating breeding behaviour is displayed by most anabantoids, i.e. bettas and gouramis, but also some catfishes and several others.You cannot believe how exciting it is to watch a pair building this delicate construction.

Breeding:
The first offspring

Many labyrinths build bubblenests, like this Siamese Fighter male (Betta splendens) taking care of his brood. One can clearly see the bubblenest. (Stock suggestion No 17)

It is incredibly exciting to watch how a bubblenest is build. The male takes in air from the water surface, cover it with mucus and releases the air in form of bubbles.

Owing to the mucus, the bubbles do not burst at the surface but stay intact and stick together so that, after a while, a "raft" or nest is build.

Under this nest the pair spawns; the eggs are then collected by the male and puffed into the nest. Eggs and larvae are taken care of until they are independent. The male tends the nest while the female defends the territory.

The well-known guppies, swordtails, platies and mollies as well as some halfbeaks belong to the group of livebearers.

The livebearing species are very popular among aquarists, and especially with beginners, as they are brightly coloured and available in many different varieties.

Females of livebearing species are fertilised by the male with the gonopodium and are pregnant most of the time when kept together with suitable partners and bear young regularly. Consequently, hobbyists can expect offspring from these species soon after setting up the tank and enjoy the sight of the first fish babies in their careers as aquarium enthusiasts.

Ornamental fishes are, of course, no "pets" in the usual sense of the word: they do not bark or miaow and, normally, they are not caressed.

A female Red-tailed Goodeid gives birth to a baby. The young comes with the tail first, swimming on its back.

But having read the preceding chapters, one can hardly say that the aquarium hobby is cold, impersonal and uninteresting.

Just like the wife of a fellow aquarist stated some time ago:

"We'll soon set up another, bigger aquarium with African cichlids, and the TV set will be moved to another room, because it is much more interesting and relaxing to watch the aquarium life than the television programme!"

Breeding:
Rearing the young

Not considering the livebearers and the mouthbrooders, the reproduction of aquarium fishes will stay the domain of experienced enthusiasts who really indulge them-selves in their hobby and also have the right setup for this advanced stage of aquarium keeping.

But - every successful breeder was a beginner once...

Therefore, I'd like to give you some advice on how to breed and rear fishes. Of course, we can only provide the most basic information; for more detailed instructions on how to breed the different species, please buy the available specialist literature, the other AQUALOG Special manuals and read the AQUALOG*news* for interesting breeding reports by experienced aquarists.

In the egg scattering species like tetras and barbs that do not take care of their brood, you need separate breeding tanks, accessory equipment and special water parameters adjusted to the species you want to breed.

For example, to provoke the spawning in certain loricariids (armoured catfishes), you have to simulate the beginning of the rainy season. But this is, in my opinion, a little bit too far advanced for beginners, and therefore, we turn to the brood caring egglayers.

In these species, breeding is easier. If you keep a pair of cavebrooders, the chances are high that you successfully breed the pair in a 60 cm tank, provided that the tank is furnished accordingly and well tended.

Open brooders are also very often successfully bred in a community tank. The basic requirement in breeding these fishes is that the tank must not be too crowded.

The parents must have the opportunity to defend the eggs against the other inhabitants when attacked; too many attackers would certainly make this task impossible.

The captions on the poster tell you whether a species belongs to the open brooders, mouthbrooders, cavebrooders etc. To be on the safe side, you transfer the brood caring egg scatterers to a separate breeding tank as soon as obviously ready-to-spawn fish have formed a pair. In such a breeding tank the offspring is, of course, most likely to survive (as they don't fall prey to any predators) and grow up to healthy, adult fish. The breeding and rearing tank has to be spacious enough and contain water with the same parameters as the main tank.

In mouthbrooders and bubble nesters you can proceed just the same if want to raise safely the majority or even all your "babies". When spawning occurs in a relatively small 60 cm tank, it is unlikely that more but a few young reach the rather safe free-swimming stage. Especially during the larva stage, the other tank inhabitants will certainly regard the fry as a nice change of the daily diet...

Many livebearers are "bad" parents and eat their fry if they can. Still, when being born the livebearer babies are very well developed and quite large.

In their natural biotopes, livebearers live in waters that are densely grown with plants so that the young can hide as soon as the left their mother's body. This way, they can escape the "cannibals". This "problem" is not apparent in small species like Cardinal and Neon tetras or Zebra danios, but larger fishes (and the own parents) are indeed life-threatening for offspring of any kind. But that's the way of nature...

If you plant your tank densely, at least some young will find a way to hide from their "enemies" and grow to beautiful, adult specimens, even more so as the quite large babies of livebearers can eat the usual foods fed to the others from the very beginning.

If this quite "natural" rearing of young does not satisfy you, you can "help" the babies by buying a special breeding trap for livebearers.

These containers are made of transparent plastic and swims at the surface due to an air cushion.

The breeding trap has two separate parts, with the top part (that contains the mother) having a narrow slit where the freshly born babies fall through, to the lower part where they are safe from their mother.

Breeding:
Breeding as a hobby

The trap is attached inside your aquarium or a respective breeding tank.

Put the pregnant female into the upper part of the trap and let her stay there for a week or so, because babies will be born continuously for several days.

The young gather in the lower part of this artificial "delivery room".

As soon as you have the feeling that no more babies are to be expected, you release the mother into the main tank and raise the young in a separate tank.

Feed the offspring with very fine dried food or fine freeze-dried food (the latter will speed up the babies' growth).

A highly pregnant female can be recognised by the size of her belly and, in most species most securely, by the conspicuously enlarged dark spot near the anal fin.

Most mouthbrooders and other brood caring species spawn only few eggs at a time.

These eggs are larger and also contain bigger yolks on which the young feed while they are growing up to the independent, free-swimming stage.

Young of these species are fed with crushed flake food as soon as they are released from their parents' care.

Feeding freshly hatched brine shrimp (*Artemia salina*) or similar freeze-dried foods one can easily raise real "champions".

Egg-scattering species that do not take care of their brood, like tetras and barbs, usually produce a large number of eggs.

Which is only too logical, as this way, the species has a chance to survive although the spawn is not defended and cared for.

Starting to feed the tiny larvae of these species is much more complicated than in larger fishes.

One needs the finest microfood, protozoans or similar small foods that cannot be seen with the naked eye.

Even infusoria are larger than the larvae of some tetras and therefore not suitable.

I recommend to refrain from breeding such difficult species.

Of course, we do not know how deeply you want to get involved in the aquarium hobby, and whether you would like to become a successful breeder or simply want to enjoy the relaxing atmosphere of an aquarium.

But - if you attempt to breed fishes at home, we wish you all the best.

To build up a stock, it is not enough to have the usual home aquarium in the living room.

You should at least have a suitable space like a garage or cellar where you can set up some tanks and start with the first cautious steps of being a fish breeder.

Our tip: Contact experienced breeders, or join a local aquarist society - its members can probably offer advice on one or the other problem.

Then simply start with your breeding efforts; you will see very soon if you have a knack for it and how well you can cope with negative experiences.

There are many specialist books on how to breed fishes; some of them are included in the list in the back of this manual.

You might even compile your own little specialist library which shouldn't miss the advisory AQUALOG manuals.

The AQUALOG-system:
Information and description

AQUALOG Lexicon

The AQUALOG team has set itself the goal to catalogue all known ornamental fishes of the world - and this task will, of course, take several years, as there are over 40 000 fish species.

Compiling an AQUALOG lexicon, we take a certain group of fishes, label all known species with code-numbers, look for the newest results of fish research about natural distribution, features and maintenance of the fishes and try to get the best photographs, often from the most remote parts of the world.

Our ingenious code-number-system labels every species with its own individual code-number which the fish keeps even if a scientific renaming occurs. And not only the species gets a number, also each variety, distinguishing locality, colour, and breeding form.

This system makes every fish absolutely distinct for everybody. With it, international communication is very easy, because a simple number crosses almost all language barriers. This is an advantage not only for dealers, but for hobbyists, too, and thus for all people involved in the aquarium hobby.

Again and again, new fish species are discovered or new varieties bred. Consequently, the number of fishes assigned to a certain group changes constantly and information from available specialist literature is only reliable within certain time limits. Thus, an identifica-tion lexicon that is up-to-date today is out-dated after as little as one year.

To give aquarists an identification 'tool' that stays up-to-date for many years, we developed our ingenious patented code-number system. When going to press, our books contain all fishes that are known to that date. All newly discovered or bred species are regularly published as either supplements or as so-called "stickups" in AQUALOGnews.

These supplementary peel-back stickers can be attached to the empty pages in the back of the books.

As you can see, we provide the latest information from specialists for hobbyists. Over the years, your AQUALOG books will 'grow' to a complete encyclopaedia on ornamental fishes, a beautiful lexicon that is never outdated and easy to use.

AQUALOGnews

AQUALOGnews is the first international newspaper for aquarists, published in four-colour print, available in either German or English language and full of the latest news from the aquatic world.

The following rubrics are included: Top Ten, Brand New, Evergreens, Technics, Terraristics, Fish Doctor and Flora. Further, there are travel accounts, breeding reports, stories about new and well-known fish etc.

The news gives us the opportunity to be highly actual, because up to one week before going to press, we can include reports and the 'hottest' available information.

This way, every six weeks a newspaper for friends of the aquarium hobby is published that makes sure to inform you about the latest 'arrivals' waiting for you at your local pet shop.

AQUALOGnews can be subscribed to and contains 40 supplementary stickers for your AQUALOG books in 12 issues. You can subscribe to the news either via your local pet shop or directly at the publishers.

Issues without stickups (print run: 80 000) are available at well-sorted pet shops. The newspaper also informs you about newly published supplements.

AQUALOG Special

The Specials series is not intended to repeat all the things that were already known twenty years ago, like 'how to build your own aquarium' - something, probably nobody practises anymore, because there is no need to do so.

We provide the latest and most important information on fish keeping and tending in precise and easily understandable language. We want to offer advice that helps you to avoid mistakes - and your fishes to live a healthy life.

We intend to win more and more friends for our beautiful and healthy (because stress-reducing!) hobby. Order our new free catalogue, where all our previous and future books are shown and described.

ISBN: 3-931702-69-3   ISBN: 3-931702-41-3   ISBN: 3-931702-34-0

Upcoming specials:

Freshwater Coral Fish: Cichlids from Lake Malawi
Freshwater Coral Fish: Cichlids from Lake Tanganjika
Majestic Discus
Shrimps and Crabs in the Freshwater Aquarium
Goldfish and Fancy Goldfish
Breathtaking Rainbows
The Colourful World of Livebearers
Impressive Big Cichlids from Central America
Amazing Dwarf Cichlids from South America
The Most Beautiful Corydoras
Freshwater Jewels: Killifishes of the Old World
Freshwater Jewels: Killifishes of the New World
Beautiful Tetras from Africa
The Most Beautiful Tetras from South America
The Most Beautiful Aquarium Plants
Beloved Monsters: The Most Bizarre Fishes
Odd Shapes (...but they are fish!)
Horror or Passion: The most beautiful Tarantulas

Popular Aquarium Fishes I: Fishes for Beginners
Popular Aquarium Fishes II: Fishes for Advanced
                             Hobbyists
Popular Aquarium Fishes III: Fishes for Experts

Decorative Aquaria :   A Malawi Biotope Tank
Decorative Aquaria :   A Tanganjika Biotope Tank
Decorative Aquaria :   An Amazonas Biotope Tank
Decorative Aquaria :   A Marine Tank for
                        Beginners
Decorative Aquaria :   A Dutch Waterplant Tank
Decorative Aquaria :   Westafrica Biotope Tank
Decorative Aquaria :   South Asia Biotope Tank
Decorative Aquaria :   Impressive Cichlids from
                        Central America
Decorative Aquaria :   Amazing Dwarf Cichlids
                        from South America
Decorative Aquaria :   An Aquaterrarium

Order your free copy of
AQUALOG*news* and
the A.C.S. programme!

Infos and news:

Verlag A.C.S. GmbH
Liebigstr. 1
D-63110 Rodgau
http://www.aqualog.de

Tel.: +49 (0) 06106 - 64 46 9 - 1
Fax: +49 (0) 06106 - 64 46 9 - 2
E-Mail: acs@aqualog.de

Index

Literature References

Magazines:

AQUALOG*news*
Verlag A.C.S. GmbH
ISSN 1430-9610

Das AQUARIUM
Birgit Schmettkamp, Verlag
ISSN 0341 - 2709

TI Magazin
Tetra Verlag
ISSN 0942 - 5160

Books:

BASLEER, G. (1996):
Bildatlas der Fischkrankheiten im
Süßwasseraquarium
Augsburg

BORK, D./MAYLAND. H.J. (1998)
Seltene Schönheiten
im Aquarium
Bornheim

GLASER U. (1998)
Fische des Jahres
„Die Highlights"
Mörfelden-Walldorf

GLASER U. (1998)
Loricariidae
Die schönsten L-Welse
Mörfelden-Walldorf

GLASER U./GLASER W. (1995)
Loricariidae - All L-Numbers
Mörfelden-Walldorf

GLASER U./GLASER W. (1996)
Southamerican Cichlids I
Mörfelden-Walldorf

GLASER U./GLASER W. (1996)
Southamerican Cichlids II
Mörfelden-Walldorf

GLASER U./SCHÄFER F./GLASER W. (1996)
Southamerican Cichlids III
Mörfelden-Walldorf

GLASER U./SCHÄFER F./GLASER W. (1996)
All Corydoras
Mörfelden-Walldorf

KASSELMANN, C. (1995)
Aquarienpflanzen
Stuttgart

MAYLAND H.J. (1998)
Southamerican Cichlids IV
Diskus und Skalare
Mörfelden-Walldorf

MAYLAND. H.J. (1995)
Mein kleines Aquarium
Hannover

MAYLAND. H.J./ BORK, D. (1997)
South American Dwarf Cichlids
Hannover

PAYSAN, K. (1996)
Beispelhafte Aquarien
Melle

REICHENBACH-KLINKE (1975)
Krankheiten und Schädigungen
der Fische
Stuttgart

SCHÄFER F./ (1997)
All Labyrinths
Mörfelden-Walldorf

SEEGERS L./ (1997)
Old World Killis I
Mörfelden-Walldorf

SEEGERS L./ (1997)
Old World Killis II
Mörfelden-Walldorf

SCHÄFER F./ KEMPKES M. (1998)
Alle Lebendgebärenden/
All Livebearers and Halfbeaks
Mörfelden-Walldorf

STALLKNECHT, H. (1996)
Freude an Aquarien
Melle

STALLKNECHT, H. (1996)
Alle Tage Jungfische
Melle

UNTERGASSER, D. (1989)
Krankheiten der Aquarienfische
Stuttgart

Symbols

In order to include as many pictures as possible, and bearing the international nature of the publication in mind, we have intentionally decided against detailed textual descriptions, replacing them by international symbols. This way, one can easily obtain the most important facts about the species and its care.

Continent of origin:

simply check the letter in front of the code-number
A = Africa **E** = Europe + North America
S = South America **X** = Asia + Australia

Age:

the last number of the code always stands
for the age of the fish in the photo:

1 = small (baby, juvenile colouration)
2 = medium (young fish / saleable size)
3 = large (half grown / good saleable size)
4 = XL (fully grown / adult)
5 = XXL (brooder)
6 = show (show-fish)

Immediate origin:

W = wild
B = bred
Z = breeding form
X = crossbreed

Size:

..cm = approximate size these fish can reach as adults.

Sex:

♂ male **♀** female **♂♀** pair

Temperature:

◁ 18-22°C (68 - 72°F) (room temperature)
▷ 22-25°C (71 -77°F) (tropical fish)
△ 24-29°C (75 - 85°F) (Discus etc)
▽ 10-22°C (50 - 72°F) cold

pH-Value:

P pH 6,5 - 7,2 no special requirements (neutral)
♭P pH 5,8 - 6,5 prefers soft, slightly acidic water
♯P ph 7,5 - 8,5 prefers hard, alkaline water

Lighting:

○ bright, plenty of light / sun
◑ not too bright
◐ almost dark

Food:

☺ omnivorous / dry food, no special requirements
☺ food specialist, live food/ frozen food
☹ predator, feed with live fish
◉ plant eater, supplement with plant food

Swimming:

⊞ no special characteristics
⬆ in upper area / surface fish
⬇ in lower area / floor fish

Aquarium setup:

only floor and stones etc.
stones / roots / crevices
plant aquarium + stones / roots

Behaviour / reproduction:

♥ keep a pair or a trio
school fish, do not keep less than 10
egglayer
livebearers / viviparous
mouthbrooder
cavebrooder
bubblenest builder
◇ algae eater / glass cleaner (roots + spinach)
◈ non aggressive fish, easy to keep (mixed aquarium)
⚠ difficult to keep, read specialist literature beforehand
🛑 warning, extremely difficult, for experienced specialists only
0 the eggs need a special care
§ protected species (WA), special license required ("CITES")

Minimum tank: capacity:

⬚ss	super small	20 - 40 cm	5 - 20 l
⬚s	small	40 - 80 cm	40 - 80 l
⬚m	medium	60 - 100 cm	80 - 200 l
⬚L	large	100 - 200 cm	200 - 400 l
⬚XL	XL	200 - 400 cm	400 - 3000 l
⬚XXL	XXL	over 400 cm	over 3000 l
			(show aquarium)

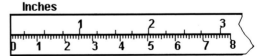

Inches

Centimeter

5

S92856-4 *Xiphophorus maculatus*
Roter Korallen-Platy / Coral Red Platy
W: Central America; B, Z, 5-6cm
Männchen mit Gonopodium / Male with gonopodium

photo: F. Teigler/A.C.S.

S92875-4 *Xiphophorus maculatus*
Blauer Platy / Blue Platy
W: Mexico / Central America; B, Z, 5-6 cm
Männchen mit Gonopodium / Male with gonopodium

photo: F. Teigler/A.C.S.

6

A43950-4 *Melanochromis auratus*
Türkisgoldbarsch / Nyasa Golden Cichlid
W: Lake Malawi / Africa; B, 8-11 cm
Erwachsene Männchen blau-schwarz / Adult males blue-black

photo: Archiv A.C.S.

A43625-5 *Maylandia greshakei „ALBINO"*
Albino Ice-Blue Malawi-Cichlid
W: Lake Malawi / Africa; B, Z, 8-10 cm
Männchen größer / Male larger

photo: Archiv A.C.S.

7

A31570-3 *Eutropiellus buffei (Etropiella debauwi)*
Afrikanischer Glaswels/ Three Striped Glass Catfish
Nigeria, Cameroun / Africa; W, 6-8 cm
Männchen schlanker / Male more elongate

photo: F. Teigler/A.C.S.

A84120-3 *Synodontis angelicus*
Perlhuhnwels / Polkadot African Catfish
Zaire-River, Congo, Cameroon / Africa; W, 10-12 cm
Männchen schlanker / Male more elongate

photo: F. Teigler/A.C.S.

8

S19755-3 *Corydoras pygmaeus*
Zwerg-Panzerwels / Pygmy Corydoras
Peru + Columbia / South America, W, 2,5-3 cm
Männchen kleiner, schlanker / Males smaller, more elongate

photo: Archiv A.C.S.

S18050-4 *Corydoras aeneus*
Metall-Panzerwels / Bronze Corydoras
W: Many countries in South America; B, 6-6,5 cm
Männchen kleiner, schlanker / Males smaller, more elongate

photo: F. Teigler/A.C.S.

S64920-4 *Poecilia sphenops*
Black Molly
W: Central America; B, Z, 5-6 cm
Männchen mit Gonopodium / Male with gonopodium

photo: F. Teigler/A.C.S.

S65105-4 *Poecilia velifera*
Segelkärpfling / Sailfin Molly
W: Yucatan, Mexico / Central America; B, Z, 8-15 cm
Männchen mit hoher Rückenflosse / Male with high dorsal fin

photo: Archiv A.C.S.

A38940-4 *Julidochromis ornatus*
Gelber Schlankcichlide / Julie
W: Lake Tanganjika / Africa; B, 7-8 cm
Männchen kleiner / Male smaller

photo: F. Teigler/A.C.S.

A48003-3 *Neolamprologus brichardi (Lamprologus)*
Prinzessin von Burundi, Feenbarsch/Lyretail Lamprologus
W: Lake Tanganjika / Africa; B, 8-10 cm
Männchen mit längeren Flossen / Male with longer fins

photo: F. Teigler/A.C.S.

A55130-4 *Pelvicachromis pulcher (kribensis)*
Purpurprachtbarsch, Königscichlide / Rainbow Cichlid
W: Nigeria / Africa; B, 8-10 cm
Weibchen kleiner, farbiger / Female smaller, more colourful

photo: F. Teigler/A.C.S.

X44701-3 *Epalzeorhynchos bicolor (Labeo)*
Feuerschwanz / Black Redtail Shark
W: Thailand / Southeast-Asia; B, 10-12 cm
Männchen kleiner, schlanker / Males smaller, more elongate

photo: Archiv A.C.S.

S19095-4 *Corydoras julii*
Leopard-Panzerwels / Leopard Corydoras
Rio Negro, Brazil / South America; W, 4,5-5 cm
Männchen kleiner, schlanker / Males smaller, more elongate

photo: F. Teigler/A.C.S.

X44755-4 *Crossocheilus siamensis (Epalzeorhynchus)*
Siam-Rüsselbarbe / Siam Algae Eater
Thailand / Southeast-Asia; W, 8-10 cm
Männchen kleiner, schlanker / Males smaller, more elongate

photo: Archiv A.C.S.

S92605-4 *Xiphophorus helleri*
Roter Schwertträger / Red Swordtail
W: Central America; B, Z, 8-10 cm
Nur Männchen mit Schwert / Female without sword

photo: Archiv A.C.S.

S92645-4 *Xiphophorus helleri*
Gold-Schwertträger / Golden Swordtail
W: Central America; B, Z, 8-10 cm
Nur Männchen mit Schwert / Female without sword

photo: Archiv A.C.S.

X11505-3 *Barbus titteya (Puntius)*
Bitterlingsbarbe / Cherry Barb
W: Sri Lanka / South-Asia; B, 4-5 cm
Männchen farbiger / Male more colourful

photo: Archiv A.C.S.

X10155-4 *Barbus conchonius (Puntius)*
Prachtbarbe / Rosy Barb
W: India / South-Asia, B, 5-6 (-12) cm
Männchen farbiger / Male more colourful

photo: F. Teigler/A.C.S.

X54005-3 *Kryptopterus minor (bicirrhis)*
Indischer Glaswels / Glass Catfish
W: Thailand, Malaysia, Indonesia / Southeast-Asia; B, 6-8 cm
Geschlechter sehr ähnlich / Sexes very similar

photo: Archiv A.C.S.

X01205-3 *Pangio semicinctus (Acanthophthalmus)*
Dornauge / Kuhlii Loach
Malaysia, Indonesia / Southeast-Asia; W, 7-8 cm
Männchen kleiner, schlanker / Males smaller, more elongate

photo: Archiv A.C.S.

S01970-3 *Ancistrus dolichopterus*
Blauer Antennenharnischwels / Bristlenose
W: Amazonas / South America; B, 10-12 cm
Männchen mit Nasententakeln / Male with bristlenose

photo: Archiv A.C.S.

S55605-3 *Otocinclus affinis*
Saugwels / Otocinclus Sucker Cat
Brazil, Peru, Venezuela / South America; W, 3,5-4 cm
Männchen kleiner, schlanker / Males smaller, more elongate

photo: Archiv A.C.S.

A

B

1

S11545-3 *Carnegiella strigata strigata*
Marmor-Beilbauch / Marbled Hatchetfish
Iquitos, Peru / South America, W, 4 cm
Männchen kleiner / Males smaller

photo: F. Teigler / A.C.S.

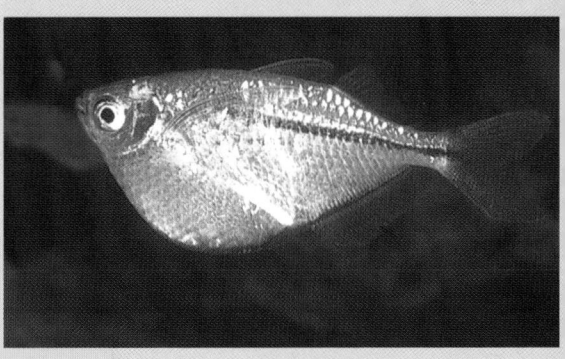

S32055-3 *Gasteropelecus sternicla*
Silber-Beilbauch / Silver Hatchetfish
Guyana, Surina, Brazil / South America, W, 5,5-6,5 cm
Männchen kleiner / Males smaller

photo: F. Teigler / A.C.S.

2

A85480-3 *Synodontis nigriventris*
Rückenschwimmender Kongo-Wels / Upsidedown-Cat
Zaire-Area / Africa; W, 5-6 cm
Männchen kleiner / Males smaller

photo: F. Teigler / A.C.S.

X90605-3 *Tanichthys albonubes*
Kardinalfisch / White Cloud Mountain Minnow
W: South-China / Asia; B, 3-4cm
Männchen kleiner, bunter / Males smaller, more colourful

photo: Archiv A.C.S.

3

X93185-4 *Trichogaster trichopterus sumatranus*
Blauer Fadenfisch / Blue Gourami
W: Sumatra / Asia; B, 13-15cm
Männchen mit spitzer Rückenflosse / Male with pointed dorsal fin

photo: Archiv A.C.S.

X93005-4 *Trichogaster leerii*
Mosaik-Fadenfisch / Pearl Gourami
W: Malaysia+Indonesia / Asia; B, 10-12 cm
Männchen mit spitzer Rückenflosse / Male with pointed dorsal fin

photo: Archiv A.C.S.

4

X28505-3 *Brachydanio rerio*
Zebra-Bärbling/Zebra-Danio
W: India / Asia; B, 4-5,5cm

S67005-3 *Prionobrama filigera*
Rotflossen-Glassalmler / Redfin-Glass-Tetra
W: Rio Paraguay, Argentina, S-Brazil / South America; B, 5-6 cm

S35015-3 *Hasemania nana*
Kupfersalmler/Copper Tetra
Brazil / South America; B, 4-5 cm
Männchen kleiner, schlanker / Males smaller, more elongate
photo: Archiv A.C.S.

S58215-3 *Paracheirodon innesi*
Neonsalmler / Neon Tetra
W: Rio Putumayo, Peru / South America; B, 3,5 -4 cm
Männchen kleiner, schlanker / Males smaller, more elongate
photo: Archiv A.C.S.

A00156-3 *Alestes longipinnis*
Afrikanischer Langflossensalmler / Longfinned Characin
Nigeria, Ghana, Togo / Africa; W, 10-12cm
Männchen mit langer Rückenflosse / Male with long dorsal fin
photo: F.Teigler/A.C.S.

A58270-4 *Phenacogrammus interruptus*
Blauer Kongosalmler / Blue Congo Tetra
W: Zaire-Area / Africa; B, 6-8 cm
Männchen mit langer Rückenflosse / Male with long dorsal fin
photo: F.Teigler/A.C.S.

X93015-4 *Trichogaster trichopterus „GOLD"*
Gold-Fadenfisch / Golden Gourami
Zuchtform / Breeding form; B, Z, 10-12 cm
Männchen mit spitzer Rückenflosse / Male with pointed dorsal fin
photo: Archiv A.C.S.

X58305-4 *Macropodus opercularis*
Paradiesfisch / Chinese Paradise Fish
W: S-China; B, 10-12cm
Männchen mit längeren Flossen / Male with longer fins
photo: U.Werner

X84245-3 *Rasbora heteromorpha*
Keilfleck-Bärbling / Harlequin
W: Malaysia, Indonesia / Asia; B, 4-4,5 cm

S39520-3 *Hyphessobrycon bentosi bentosi*
Schmucksalmler / Rosy-Tetra
W: Guyana, Amazonas / South America; B, 3,5-4cm

S58205-3 *Paracheirodon axelrodi*
Roter Neon / Cardinal Tetra
W: Brazil / South America; W, 4,5 cm
Männchen kleiner, schlanker / Males smaller, more elongate
photo: Archiv A.C.S.

S39670-3 *Hyphessobrycon herbertaxelrodi*
Schwarzer Neon / Black Neon Tetra
W: Brazil, Paraguay / South America; B, 4 cm
Männchen kleiner, schlanker / Males smaller, more elongate
photo: Archiv A.C.S.

S39620-3 *Hyphessobrycon erythrostigma*
Kirschflecksalmler / Bleeding Heart Tetra
upper Amazonas-Area, Peru / South America; W, 5-6 cm
Männchen mit langer Rückenflosse / Male with long dorsal fin
Photo: Archiv A.C.S.

S39580-3 *Hyphessobrycon callistus „minor"*
Blutsalmler / Blood Tetra
Zuchtform / Breeding form; B, 3,5-4 cm
Männchen kleiner, schlanker / Males smaller, more elongate
photo: F. Teigler/A.C.S.

X18520-4 *Betta splendens „FANTAIL"*
Schleier-Kampffisch / Siamese Fighter
Zuchtform / Breeding form; B, Z, 5-6 cm
Weibchen mit normalen Flossen / Female with normal fins
photo: M. Smith

X40215-4 *Colisa lalia*
Zwerg-Fadenfisch / Dwarf Gourami
W: India; B, 5-6 cm
Männchen farbiger / Male more colourful
photo: Archiv A.C.S.

S72115-4 *Pterophyllum scalare*
Segelflosser / Angelfish "Leopard-Gold"
W: Guyana + Amazonas / South America; B, Z, 10-15 cm
Geschlechter sehr ähnlich / Sexes very similar

S54225-4 *Nematobrycon palmeri*
Kaisertetra / Emperor Tetra
W: Columbia / South America; W, 4,5-5 cm
Männchen mit größeren Flossen / Males with longer fins

H

photo: Archiv A.C.S.

S52020-4 *Microgeophagus ramirezi (Papiliochromis)*
Schmetterlingsbuntbarsch / Butterfly-Dwarf-Cichlid
W: Venezuela+Columbia / South America; B, 6-7 cm
Weibchen kleiner farbiger / Female smaller more colourful

photo: Archiv A.C.S.

S52615-3 *Moenkhausia sanctaefilomenae*
Rotaugen-Moenkhausia/Red-Eye-Moenkhausia
W: Peru,Bolivia,W-Brazil, Paraguay / South America; B, 5-6 cm
Männchen kleiner, schlanker / Males smaller, more elongate

photo: Archiv A.C.S.

S53415-3 *Nannostomus beckfordi*
Längsband-Ziersalmler/ Golden Pencilfish
Guyana+Brazil / South America; W, 5-6cm
Männchen kleiner, schlanker / Males with white fin tips

photo: Archiv A.C.S.

S39760-3 *Hyphessobrycon pulchripinnis*
Zitronensalmer / Lemon Tetra
W: Tocantins-Area, Brazil / South America; B, 4-4,5 cm
Männchen kleiner, schlanker / Males smaller, more elongate

G

photo: Archiv A.C.S.

42805-4 *Inpaichthys kerry*
Königssalmler / Blue Emperor
Amazonas-Area / South America; B, 4cm
Männchen größer farbiger / Males bigger more colourful

photo: Archiv A.C.S.

S60805-3 *Petitella georgiae*
Rotkopfsalmler / Rummynose-Tetra
Iquitos, Peru + Brazil / South America; W, 4-5 cm
Männchen kleiner, schlanker / Males smaller, more elongate

photo: Archiv A.C.S.

S35780-3 *Hemigrammus rodwayi (armstrongi)*
Gold-Tetra
Guyana, Columbia / South America; W, 4-5 cm
Männchen kleiner, schlanker / Males smaller, more elongate

photo: Archiv A.C.S.

S35670-3 *Hemigrammus erythrozonus*
Glühlichtsalmler / Glowlight Tetra
W: Essequibo-River Guyana / South America; B, 4 cm
Männchen kleiner, schlanker / Males smaller, more elongate

S64385-4 *Poecilia reticulata (Lebistes)*
Schleier-Guppy / Veiltail-Guppy "King-Kobra Red"
W: South + Central America; B, Z, 5-6 cm
Weibchen größer, farbloser / Female larger, less colourful
photo: F. Teigler/A.C.S.

S64378-4 *Poecilia reticulata (Lebistes)*
Schleier-Guppy / Veiltail-Guppy "King-Kobra Gold"
W: South + Central America; B, Z, 5-6 cm
Weibchen größer, farbloser / Female larger, less colourful
photo: F. Teigler/A.C.S.

X10775-4 *Barbus nigrofasciatus (Puntius)*
Purpurkopfbarbe / Black Ruby Barb
W: Sri Lanka / South-Asia; B, 5-7 cm
Männchen farbiger / Male more colourful
photo: Archiv A.C.S.

X11305-3 *Barbus tetrazona (Puntius)*
Sumatrabarbe / Sumatra Barb
W: Sumatra, Borneo, Indonesia / Southeast-Asia; B, 5-6 cm
Männchen farbiger / Male more colourful
photo: Archiv A.C.S.

A37850-3 *Hymenochirus boettgeri*
Zwergkrallenfrosch / African Underwater Dwarf-Frog
W: Zaire-Area / Africa; B, 3-4 cm
Männchen kleiner, schlanker / Males smaller, more elongate
photo: F. Teigler/A.C.S.

X27805-4 *Botia striata*
Zebra-Schmerle / Zebra Loach
India / South Asia; W, 7-9 cm
Männchen kleiner, schlanker / Males smaller, more elongate
photo: F. Teigler/A.C.S.

S60115-3 *Peckoltia pulcher*
Gebänderter Zwergschilderwels / Clown Sucker
Rio Negro, Brazil, Columbia / South America; W, 5,5-6 cm
Männchen kleiner, schlanker / Males smaller, more elongate
photo: E. Schraml/A.C.S.

X27355-4 *Botia macracanthus*
Prachtschmerle / Clown-Loach
Indonesia, Sumatra, Borneo / Southeast-Asia; W, 12-20 cm
Männchen kleiner, schlanker / Males smaller, more elongate
photo: Archiv A.C.S.